ALA ☀ **Fundamentals Series**

# Fundamentals of
# Library
# Supervision

D1166630

*Joan Giesecke and Beth McNeil*

**AMERICAN LIBRARY ASSOCIATION**
Chicago    2005

While extensive effort has gone into ensuring the reliability of information appearing in this book, the publisher makes no warranty, express or implied, on the accuracy or reliability of the information, and does not assume and hereby disclaims any liability to any person for any loss or damage caused by errors or omissions in this publication.

Design and composition by ALA Editions in Galliard and Optima using QuarkXPress 5.0 on a PC platform

Printed on 50-pound white offset, a pH-neutral stock, and bound in 10-point cover stock by McNaughton & Gunn

The paper used in this publication meets the minimum requirements of American National Standard for Information Sciences—Permanence of Paper for Printed Library Materials, ANSI Z39.48-1992. ∞

**Library of Congress Cataloging-in-Publication Data**

Giesecke, Joan.
    Fundamentals of library supervision / by Joan Giesecke and Beth McNeil.
        p.   cm. — (ALA fundamentals series)
    Includes bibliographical references and index.
    ISBN 0-8389-0895-0 (alk. paper)
    1. Library personnel management—United States. 2. Supervision of employees.
  I. McNeil, Beth. II. Title. III. Series.
    Z682.2.U5G54 2005
    023′.9—dc22                                 2004024654

Printed in the United States of America

09   08   07   06        5   4   3   2

# CONTENTS

# FIGURES

# PREFACE

Management used to be simple. The manager or supervisor told employees what to do and employees did what they were told. That world does not exist today. Today's managers, supervisors, team leaders, project managers, and unit heads face a more complex environment. Managers need to balance production goals with concern for people issues in a continually changing environment. The workplace and the workforce are different. Managers may now find they have four generations of staff, each with its own characteristics and needs. Each group responds to different management styles. More women are in management roles as well, bringing a different perspective to the administration of the organization.

The legal environment is also more complex, with laws addressing discrimination, sexual harassment, health issues, and other personnel issues. Today's supervisor needs to keep up with legal changes if he or she is to avoid legal challenges.

While our world is more complicated, it is also more exciting. Managers have more flexibility in how they structure their units or organizations. They have more options for delegating tasks, establishing goals, and encouraging staff development. They can build high-powered teams that surpass traditionally structured units.

How can supervisors and managers create an exciting environment? Many of the fundamentals of management that lead to a productive workplace are just basic common sense. Others require taking a new view of management and letting go of the idea of central control.[1]

In this book we cover the fundamentals of good management and bring together practical advice from experts, using basic commonsense approaches to solving today's management challenges. Whether you are a new supervisor just getting started or an experienced manager, you will find that the topics included here provide you with an overview and foundation for the tasks and challenges of being a manager.

The topics covered include how to get started as a supervisor or manager, how to create a positive working environment, how to manage teams, working with a diverse workforce, and recognizing fundamental legal issues that are part of today's workplace. Practical skills that are covered include hiring, interviewing, orienting, and appraising employees; managing rewards; and planning and organizing work. Project management, meeting management, and communication skills are also covered. The examples and stories in this book are composites created from a variety of experiences and organizations. All names, circumstances, and details have been altered, and any resemblance to real people is coincidental.

If you enjoy bringing people together and helping them do their best, you are ready to be a manager. Enjoy the complexities and challenges that make up this very exciting world.

## NOTE

1. Camilla Alire, "Two Intriguing Practices to Library Management Theory," *Library Administration and Management* 18, no. 1 (winter 2004): 39–41.

# 1
# Today's Workplace

Today's managers face a workplace that is significantly different from the one that existed even twenty years ago. Today's world is more fast-paced, and change is a way of life. Organizations face new competition, changing technology, mergers and acquisitions, changing consumer expectations, and economic instability. They work in a global environment with potential suppliers and customers located anywhere. Jobs are being outsourced to offshore companies and third world nations. Multinational companies are learning how to blend cultures and develop management structures that can be successful in multiple environments. Technological changes affect all aspects of business, from financial systems to human resources and knowledge-base systems. Just trying to keep up with the many changes in how technology can be used is a full-time job. Furthermore, managers are faced with the instability that can result from mergers and acquisitions, as well as from the blending of different types of organizations within the same industry. Managing becomes more of a challenge when you're not sure if the top management of the company is arranging a restructuring or planning to sell the company to another owner. Long-range plans quickly become short-term strategies for survival if you don't think you have a long time frame in which to protect your own career. To compound these uncertainties, today's managers also face an unstable economic environment in which budget reductions, downsizing, and the restructuring of financial plans are facts of life. Externally, organizations face the challenge of new expectations from customers who want to customize anything they can and want everything quickly. Satisfying customer demands when those demands are always changing compounds the challenges involved in planning and organizing work for maximum effectiveness and efficiency.

## Trends

Libraries are not immune to these forces, and library managers need to understand how these forces and other trends affect their organizations.[1]

*Competition.* Libraries face competition from a variety of sources, including the most obvious one, the Internet and the World Wide Web. Today's students, consumers, and company employees are more likely to try the Internet first for information than they are to check with a librarian. Library patrons can also be found studying in bookstores with cafés and comfortable seating rather than in public, school, or academic libraries. Library managers need to understand this new world of competition if they are to position their libraries to remain a vital part of their communities or organizations.

Competition is leading librarians into becoming marketing managers who must learn how to advertise and market their services. No longer can libraries afford to sit back and simply assume that everyone knows what libraries can contribute to the community. Instead, librarians need to develop plans to explain why libraries are still needed and how they play a vital role in the information-rich world we live in. The American Library Association's "@ Your Library" campaign is one of many ways libraries can market their services and advertise their worth.

*Technology.* Changing technology is now a way of life in today's libraries. The library manager who waits to find the perfect system before implementing new technologies will not be successful. Librarians have to become risk takers, trying new technologies even though the results are not guaranteed. Managers must also let go of the idea that once a decision on technology has been made and the hardware and software have been purchased, they can keep that technology for a long time. Hardware and software change regularly, and libraries must find ways to keep current if the library is to remain vital to its patrons. Finding the funds to upgrade workstations on a three-year cycle, for example, will change how budgets are structured and how priorities are set.

Changes in technology also affect internal organizational structures. With networked resources and online systems available in many libraries, managers may find that their staff includes employees who want to telecommute rather than work on-site. Supervising these employees takes careful planning and creativity to ensure that productivity measures are met and that these staff feel a part of the overall unit or department. The use of technology also brings ergonomic concerns to the workplace, with supervisors now needing to address issues of safety in the workplace, such as workstation arrangements that will minimize the chances of staff developing carpal tunnel syndrome or other health problems. While formerly any table or chair might do, today's staffers who spend all day working at computers need a work space that can be adjusted to meet their individual needs.

Technology also affects how decisions can be made. Supervisors may now have access to a variety of data on workload, productivity, and customer satisfaction that they might not have had twenty years ago.

*Mergers and acquisitions.* While most libraries don't think about mergers as a major force in the library field, similar changes in their organizational structures are indeed occurring. Public and school libraries are being blended in the same space. Corporations are centralizing information services, eliminating smaller local collections and services. Academic libraries are closing branches and building virtual libraries instead of physical collections to serve dispersed populations. Granted, these same types of changes have occurred at various times in the history of libraries. But today, with economic uncertainties and the changing information world, managers may face situations that they never thought would affect their institutions.

*Customer expectations.* Libraries know that customer expectations have changed. Customers want access to a wide variety of information resources and services at times that are convenient for them. Libraries that are not customer-focused will not be supported and will find that their funding suffers.

*Economic uncertainty.* Libraries are all too familiar with the problems of budget and staffing reductions. In tough economic times, libraries may be seen as less central to the core mission of an organization, less central to the core activities of a school, less important to a state, county, or city government that has to pay for mandated initiatives and social programs.

*Changing workforce.* Perhaps the most noticeable trend is the changing demographics of the United States. The population is becoming more diverse. Libraries need to learn to recruit and retain staff from a variety of ethnic and racial backgrounds. Another change in demographics is the expanding number of generations in the workplace, with four generations of workers now a part of many of our institutions. Supervisors can no longer assume that all employees will behave and react to the environment in the same way. Many of today's newer employees are interested first in what they can get out of a job rather than in how they can contribute to it. Supervisors need to think about how to build partnerships with staff to get the work done rather than simply giving orders and having staff carry out those orders.

*Global economy.* While many libraries may think of themselves as local institutions, libraries are still connected to and influenced by the global economy. As a result of mergers in the publishing field, libraries are buying many of their reference and scholarly resources from companies headquartered in Europe and other regions. Acquisition budget planning has to include the impact of exchange rates as well as that of inflation.

Libraries and publishers are also taking advantage of the global economy by outsourcing digitization work to countries such as China and India where labor costs are lower than in the United States. Partnerships are being created, too, as libraries here join with ones in other countries to provide online real-time reference assistance on a 24-hour basis. These partnerships are helping libraries expand their services to meet the demand for service in a 24/7 world.

Today's library managers and supervisors need to be aware of all these trends and how they will affect their own institutions and organizations. Every manager has to understand the big picture of the information field if he or she is to be successful in an environment of change.

## Changing Roles of Managers and Supervisors

Not only are the organizations we work in changing, but the roles of supervisors are also changing. In the mid-twentieth century, the manager's role could be described by the acronym POSDCoRB, which stands for:

*Planning.* Managers were responsible for determining organization goals and deciding how the organization should meet those goals.

*Organizing*. Managers determined how the work would be divided among organizational units and decided what procedures would be used to accomplish those tasks.

*Staffing*. Managers were responsible for the personnel decisions in their units, including hiring and evaluating staff.

*Directing*. Managers directed the work of others, deciding who would complete which tasks.

*Coordinating*. Managers coordinated activities between units. Staff were responsible only for work within their own units.

*Reporting*. Managers were responsible for reporting on unit accomplishments and keeping upper management informed about unit progress.

*Budgeting*. Managers were responsible for the unit's budget, determining how resources would be divided and monitoring that budgets were met.

While these roles still exist in our organizations, it is more likely that in today's environment these activities are shared between the supervisors and the staff. The supervisor is now more of a coach than a director, and more of a facilitator than a commander. New roles for supervisors include recognizing and recruiting talent, teaching staff new skills and promoting learning, understanding the organization's culture, and understanding organizational power.

*Talent*. Successful supervisors are learning new ways to recruit staff. They are learning that they need to recruit talent and ability rather than looking only at skills. Supervisors know they can teach skills to talented employees easier than they can teach talent to someone. Without the key talents and abilities needed to do a job, a staff member is unlikely to excel. In today's job market, where recruiting is very competitive, it is important to recruit the best staff possible so that the unit can succeed and grow.

*Promoting learning*. Most staff today want a job that provides personal satisfaction, one where they can control their own destinies, and where they have a voice in what happens.[2] In organizations that promote learning and encourage staff development, staff members are more likely to find the satisfaction they seek. Supervisors who promote a partnership approach to the management of the unit are more likely to create an environment where staff have input in the unit and are more likely to feel appreciated for their efforts.

*Organizational culture.* Successful supervisors understand the culture of the organization in which they operate. Supervisors need to know how the organization measures success, how rewards are determined, how mistakes are handled, how decisions are made, and how risk is tolerated. They also need to understand the time frame in which the organization operates. Some libraries, for example, work on a semester system, some on the school year, and some on the fiscal year. These time frames affect how objectives are measured and how the pace of the work is likely to be set.

Supervisors can learn an organization's culture by listening carefully to others, observing how things are done, keeping an open mind about work-flow and processes, observing who succeeds and why, and remembering to look at the big picture beyond their own units. Setting aside time to reflect on organizational activities and keeping notes on what works and what does not work will help identify the key elements in the culture.

*Power.* Power is a natural part of any organization. Supervisors should review the organizational chart to see how their units fit into the overall structure and fit with each other. It also helps to identify what activities are not reflected on the organizational chart and then learn how these functions are dispersed in the organization. Understanding relationships will also help in identifying organizational politics. It helps, for example, to know if one's colleagues were sorority sisters or fraternity brothers. Do they belong to the same groups? Do these people form an alliance in the organization? How does the distribution of power in the organization relate to the political relationships? Thinking explicitly about the organization and reflecting upon what goes on inside it will give supervisors a better chance of developing ways to work that are successful and are rewarded.

## Changing Competencies

Managers and supervisors need to develop a variety of competencies beyond technical expertise to succeed in their job with these new roles and responsibilities. The soft skills of human resources management, team-building, and leadership are the foundation of successful management at all levels of an organization. Plan on putting the following competencies to work daily as you develop your skills as a manager.[3]

> *Interpersonal skills.* Supervision is about creating relationships. Good people skills are a must.

*Communication skills.* Verbal and written communication skills are crucial.

*Problem-solving and decision-making.* Learning to analyze data and using that data to resolve problems will help you work effectively. Using good judgment is also a key success factor.

*Initiative.* Taking the initiative, anticipating needs, and taking action are the signs of a good supervisor.

*Delegation.* Learning to appropriately delegate the right tasks to the right people is a skill that is often overlooked. Take time to learn how to delegate effectively.

*Time management.* Managing your own time as well as the time of your staff will make your unit more successful and able to complete assigned projects and tasks.

*Meetings management.* Much of the work in today's organizations is done through groups and teams. Knowing how to run an efficient and effective meeting will make your groups more effective. Ensuring that meetings are not seen as an alternative to work or as a waste of time and effort is an important skill.

*Customer service.* Know the needs of your patrons, your internal customers, and your external constituencies, and be sure everyone in your unit is focused on how they can meet those needs. Service is everyone's business.

## Conclusion

Change has become a way of life for the library and information field. While the core functions of libraries—providing an organized collection of materials and providing assistance in using those materials—remain the same, how libraries fulfill those functions is being transformed. Technological advances make it possible for libraries to provide access to a wide range of materials that no single library owns. Libraries can serve customers from around the world as easily as they serve the patrons who enter their buildings.

In such a world, managers in today's libraries must embrace change. The management strategies that worked many years ago are no longer successful in today's volatile environment. Managers and supervisors need to be aware of the many trends that impact the library field and learn how to bring the best of these changes into their units and organizations. Successful managers will be those who have learned to navigate in the white water of the library and information field while supervising employees who make herding cats look easy by comparison.

## NOTES

1. For an overview of current trends and their impact on the library field, see *The 2003 OCLC Environmental Scan: Pattern Recognition* (Dublin, Ohio: OCLC, 2004).

2. Gary McClain and Deborah S. Romaine, *The Everything Managing People Book* (Avon, Mass.: Adams Media, 2002), 11.

3. William A. Salmon, *The New Supervisor's Survival Manual* (New York: AMACOM, 1999), 5–7.

# 2
# Becoming a Manager

I t was Sally's first day as the supervisor of the circulation unit in her library. Sally was now in charge of her old unit and was feeling quite confident. She knew the circulation function quite well, was very knowledgeable about the policies, and was used to handling problems. Her previous unit head had left the running of the unit to Sally whenever he was unavailable. Sally was set, or so she thought. Her day started with a call to come to the circulation desk to talk to an unhappy patron. Sally had handled these kinds of problems before and was not concerned about the upcoming encounter. On her way to the desk, Tom, a member of the department and Sally's good friend, stopped her, wanting to know what Sally was going to do about the evening student who was not showing up for work. When was Sally going to take care of this problem, he wanted to know. Sally told Tom she would get to it later. Tom left, mumbling how you couldn't trust supervisors to take action. While Sally resolved the patron problem, she was handed a stack of budget papers and told she needed to get the staff budget to balance today. No one had done the monthly reports for a while and the budget was not balanced. Sally wondered why Jane hadn't been taking care of this, as it was Jane's job to monitor the budget and to alert the unit head to any problems or concerns. By now Sally was wondering what had happened to all the supportive colleagues she had yesterday before she became the unit head, and why it now seemed that no one was doing their job. Welcome to the world of supervision and management.

If this day sounds intriguing, you are thinking like a manager. Sally is quickly discovering that management is not about technical skills. Rather, it is about helping others accomplish their tasks, solving problems, developing staff, and creating a positive working environment. Sally has her work cut out for her. She must change her perspective, learn to see the unit differently, and learn how her job has now changed. She could use some training, advice, and help.

Let's explore what it takes to be the supervisor, head, or manager of a unit, department, or organization.

## Competencies

What are the core competencies for today's supervisors and managers? What are the skills, knowledge, and personal attributes that contribute to your success as a manager? If you think that the ability to give commands and control your unit will make you successful, you will be disappointed. Today's supervisors must move beyond the command and control mentality to develop skills in coaching, facilitation, and negotiation. You will need to be customer-focused, able to support and implement change in response to the changing information environment, and able to work in or lead teams and groups, while ensuring that your unit is productive and meets organizational goals and objectives.

Supervisory or managerial competencies can be divided into several categories.[1] Key skills that are the foundation for any position include technical competence, oral and written communication skills, and time management skills. In addition, all members of the organization should support diversity, demonstrate flexibility, and exhibit self-awareness.

Next, supervisors need good problem-solving and decision-making skills, and be able to manage conflict and to build teams. Supervisors also need to demonstrate personnel management skills when it comes to coaching and developing staff, setting standards and expectations, and conducting performance reviews.

As one advances in management, planning and budgeting skills become more important. Negotiating among units or departments also becomes part of one's role. Finally, thinking about the organization as a whole and working to develop and achieve organizational goals round out the manager's role.

Supervisors not only need to demonstrate these competencies themselves, but are also responsible for coaching staff to help them develop these important skills.

## Myths vs. Reality

Besides building new competencies, supervisors need to let go of a number of myths about management that no longer apply to today's workplace.[2]

*Myth:* You are in charge of everything. *Reality:* If you think about this statement, you will realize that you cannot be in charge of every detail in your unit. Staff continually make decisions about their tasks, procedures, and work. If they did not make decisions, they would not be doing their jobs. As a manager you are responsible for seeing that the work is done, and while you want to be sure you pitch in and help when needed, you are not doing your staff any favors if you try to do their work in addition to your own.

*Myth:* You cannot trust your staff. *Reality:* This myth assumes that staff are not going to do their jobs well and that management must spend time preventing poor performance. This attitude is not helpful in today's workplace, where building motivated teams of staff who take pride in their work is an important part of creating a productive, positive environment.

*Myth:* You cannot show emotion as a manager. *Reality:* The stoic leader may work well in the movies, but is not helpful in today's workplace. You should be objective when gathering facts, dealing with complaints, or investigating important issues. But you can also be happy, laugh, and enjoy a good joke with your staff. While you need to control your emotions and be sure you are being professional, you are still human and can show appropriate emotions.

*Myth:* You must always defend your staff. *Reality:* Perhaps one of the hardest things to learn as a new manager is that you need to support your staff and still recognize when performance issues have to be addressed. For example, if Sally in the circulation unit is told by her boss that patrons are complaining about the poor treatment they receive at the desk, then Sally needs to investigate the complaint and work to improve the service in the department rather than spend time defending her staff to her boss without knowing if the complaints are valid or not.

*Myth:* You always have to be right. *Reality:* As a manager, you need to learn to admit when you've made a mistake and take action to correct the problem. If you assume you must always be right, then you may ignore information that runs counter to your own beliefs. You also need to learn when to compromise and back down from a position that is no longer valid. Learning to see the big picture and recognizing when you can learn from others are an important part of being a manager.

## Roles

Letting go of these ideas about management will help you, as a supervisor, be open to taking on new roles and approaches to managing your unit. As a supervisor, you will have a number of new roles.[3] These roles include:

- mentor to your staff
- facilitator for managing conflict
- monitor of your unit's performance
- coordinator of projects
- planner for your unit
- creator working productively with your staff
- broker and negotiator for your unit
- innovator for managing change

## Style

To carry out these roles, Sally will need to develop an appropriate management style. At first, Sally may think that success will come as long as everyone likes her. All she needs to do is keep people happy. But if Sally follows this path, she will soon find that a happy staff is not necessarily a productive staff. Sally may also think that the same skills that make a good parent make a good supervisor. But treating her staff as one would treat children will not be effective either. The workplace is populated with adults and Sally needs to treat her staff as adults.

Management styles can be described in terms of staff concern and task concern.[4] A manager who is concerned with tasks but not concerned with people will be very autocratic. This command and control approach, common in the early twentieth century, was a one-way process where decisions were made by the manager and staff needs were ignored. Minimal work got done and the environment did nothing to foster excellence. Today's staff are more likely to rebel and leave rather than stay in a stifling work environment.

A manager who is concerned with staff but not concerned with tasks is out to win a popularity contest. This manager makes decisions to make people happy. Conflicts are smoothed over rather than resolved. While staff may be happy, they are not likely to be challenged to do their best.

A manager who avoids both task and people issues basically abdicates any responsibility for the unit. Here there is little or no communication, conflict is avoided, and only safe decisions are made. The absentee manager leaves the unit to fend for itself.

Finally, the manager who is concerned about both people and productivity will seek to create an environment that encourages people to do their best. Communication is two-way, conflicts are resolved, and staff are encouraged to grow and develop. These managers are most likely to create a positive working environment.

To be effective, Sally needs to develop a style that balances concern for tasks with concern for people. If and when she can balance these two elements, she will be more likely to succeed.

As Sally finishes her first day, she may find the list of roles, skills, and abilities overwhelming. How can Sally begin to establish herself as a supervisor even as she works to develop other skills needed to do the job?

## The Manager's View

One of the things that Sally has to learn as a supervisor is that her view or perspective on the organization needs to change. She is no longer one of the staff members. She needs to have an understanding of the whole unit and how her unit fits into the organization. She needs to develop relations with other supervisors, with her staff, and with her boss.

Sally will find that a manager's job is filled with ambiguity. It is an open-ended job that never seems to end. Facing multiple, unrelated problems ranging from the insignificant to the important is part of a typical manager's day. Sally will find that a manager's job is no longer about being a producer of services. Nor will Sally be an expert for a particular service or task. Rather, she will find she needs to know a little about a lot of tasks. Breadth replaces depth of knowledge. Therefore, Sally must learn to rely on her staff to be the experts. She will need to trust them to know the intricacies of each task while she tries to understand how all the tasks fit together. Sally will come to see that management is a position of interdependence, because managers need to guide their staff to excel even as they depend on them to make the unit a success.[5]

Many new managers may be surprised at how their view must change if they are to be successful.

As Sally is solving problems and handling daily crises or putting out fires, she needs to get to know her staff from the perspective of a supervisor. As a new supervisor, it is important to get to know each staff member as an individual. In the first few weeks on the job, Sally should set time aside to meet with each staff member in order to listen to their concerns. This is not the time for Sally to lecture. Rather, this is Sally's best opportunity to establish a new working relationship with each member of her unit. In these conversations, Sally asks open-ended questions about each person's job. This will help encourage staff to share their ideas and concerns. Sally can find out what people like about their jobs, what things are challenging to them, and what things they might like to see changed. Sally will want to keep the conversation friendly and work-related. This is not informal social conversation. It is an important work-related conversation that will help Sally, as a supervisor, begin to understand the intricacies and complexities of her unit.

## Building a Relationship with Your Boss

Sally also needs to have a series of conversations with her boss in order to learn how she fits into the overall organization. As a circulation manager, Sally may well be part of an access services department. She will want to find out how her unit's work affects the work of other units in the department. For example, if interlibrary loan is part of the department, but the circulation desk is the pickup location for interlibrary loan materials, then Sally will want to confirm what the expectations are for her unit regarding interlibrary loan materials. Sally will also want to clarify performance expectations with her boss. To continue this example, Sally needs to know how quickly her unit needs to process interlibrary loan returns. Clarifying expectations in the beginning will help Sally set a positive tone for working with her boss.

In establishing a working relationship with your new boss, think about the kind of employee you want working for you and determine how you can be that same type of employee for your boss. Key characteristics of a productive employer-employee relationship include the following:[6]

*Supportive.* Look for ways to support your boss, your organization, and your organization's policies and procedures. Think about what you can do to ensure that policies are implemented in your unit and that your unit is contributing to the organization's goals.

*Positive.* Bring a positive and respectful attitude to work. While your boss is not always right, and you don't want to follow him or her blindly, you will want to begin with the assumption that the boss knows what he or she is doing. A positive attitude also includes watching your own moods. While we are not likely to be cheery every day, it is important to not pout about every little mishap. An even-tempered approach to the workplace will go a long way to creating a positive, productive environment and a good working relationship with your boss.

*Good work habits.* You set the tone for your unit. When you arrive on time, don't take excessively long breaks, and keep a neat work area, you are sending a signal to your boss that you care about your job. You are also sending the same signal to your unit.

*Willingness to learn.* In today's changing information environment, it is crucial that we are always ready and willing to learn new things. Look for ways to increase knowledge of your job, your unit, and your organization. You can help your unit stay up-to-date with this changing field while showing your boss that you care about improving your unit.

*Complete assigned work on time.* While you spend a lot of time as a supervisor building relationships and interacting with your staff, it is also important to be sure that assigned tasks are completed. When your boss asks for a report or paperwork is due, get it done on time.

*Work well with others.* Your boss will look to you to build good working relationships with other supervisors in the department and in the organization. Look for ways to build networks and avoid the "us vs. them" syndrome.

## Building a Working Relationship with Your Peers

Sally also needs to begin building working relationships with her peers. Her peers are other supervisors in the unit and in the organization. This is Sally's new group of colleagues. If Sally sees her peers as competitors, she will find it difficult to build supportive relationships. She may see the actions of other units as threats to her own group. She may become defensive around other managers. Such an approach will likely lead to conflict and failure.

Sally will soon learn that her peers are her main support group. Other supervisors can provide advice on how to handle problems, how the organization functions, and how to succeed in the organization. They can help Sally see things from a different perspective and can help her formulate plans.

Unfortunately, some colleagues will not be interested in creating a positive working environment. They may be disillusioned, long-term employees who resist change. Sally will need to recognize this negative behavior and avoid letting someone else's negative view of the organization influence her own attitude. Sally cannot change these people, but she can take steps to prevent them from spreading their negative view to her unit.

As Sally develops a good working relationship with her peers and builds a lateral team in the organization, she will be better able to expand her view of the organization and work to integrate her unit into the department or institution.

## Learning the Job

While you are building working relationships with your staff, your boss, and your peers, you will also be learning the tasks that are part of your job. Even though you are an expert in some areas (or you would not have been given the job), you still need to learn these tasks from a manager's viewpoint. You will want to understand and learn all the details you may have missed as an employee or staff member. Now is the time to learn from your predecessor and your colleagues.

### *Your Predecessor*

If you can meet with your predecessor, you will find that you can gather valuable information about your unit. Your predecessor can provide a unique view of the unit and provide insights into why the unit functions as it does.

However, you will want to examine the information critically. You were hired to help the unit grow and improve. You will want to establish your own approach and style. Nonetheless, the information you receive can be useful if interpreted with careful judgment.

You may be facing a situation where you were brought in to make changes because your predecessor was not successful. In such a case, you may still want to meet with your predecessor, but recognize that the person may not be very objective about the organization.

If you can meet with your predecessor, direct the conversation to get to the information that will be most helpful to you. Subjects to raise include the following:[7]

*Department structure.* Ask what works and what does not work about the current structure.

*Mission and goals.* Learn about your predecessor's view of the unit's mission and goals. How well is the unit meeting its goals?

*Personnel strengths and challenges.* Find out what personnel issues you will need to address. Learn how your predecessor views the staff. Then remember that you will want to make your own assessment.

*Budget.* Learn how the budget was developed. What is included in it and what is missing? What resources are needed for the unit?

*Committee assignments.* Are there particular committee meetings you should attend? How are decisions made? What is your likely role?

*Hidden problems.* Can your predecessor alert you to hidden land mines in the unit? What pitfalls do you need to avoid?

The information you gather in this conversation can be a helpful guide. But remember that your predecessor may have a hidden agenda. Be sure to weigh the information you get against other information you gather as you meet with your staff and colleagues.

### Office Files

Another important source of information about the unit or department is the unit's operations manuals and files. From this written documentation you will learn how tasks are supposed to be done. You can find out about policies and procedures, paperwork, and forms. While you will find that there are some variations in how tasks are actually done, the manuals will help you learn how the tasks should be done.

*Reports.* Annual reports, committee minutes, and task force reports are also a rich source of information. These historical documents will help you understand the origin and development of your unit. You will also learn what problems have been solved and which ones keep reappearing. If you cannot find reports for your unit, ask your staff if they have copies you could borrow. Check to see if your organization has an archive of historical documents, and see if you can find unit reports there. Usually someone will have copies of some of the reports you need. Ask others for help in finding these documents.

*Personnel files.* The official personnel files will give you background information on each member of your unit. You will also see how staff have been evaluated, what problems have been addressed, and what successes have been celebrated. You may find it more effective to talk to each staff member first and begin to form your own judgments before reading past performance reviews. You will want to make sure you are being open and objective as you begin to learn about your staff. You will also want to ensure that you are not unduly influenced by your predecessor's view of the staff.

By reviewing the written documentation available about your unit, you will learn how tasks are done, how policies and procedures are carried out, and how the unit documentation is created and saved. All this information will help you learn your job as you learn about the group you now manage.

## Conclusion

At the end of Sally's first day, she sat down to take stock. She handled patron complaints, found out the budget was only slightly out of balance, and wondered what to do about the student who was not showing up for work. Sally realized that no one was going to create an orientation sched-ule for her or tell her how to do her job. Instead, Sally created her first major "to do" list and thought about how she should proceed with her job.

Her list included a schedule for the next few months. On her list, Sally put the following:

> Hold a fifteen-minute meeting each morning with staff to review the work for the day, as a way to decrease the number of unexpected crises and events.
>
> Schedule individual meetings with staff members. Do two per day.
>
> Set aside one to two hours each day to read files, documents, and reports.

Schedule a meeting with her boss.

Schedule meetings with other supervisors. Try for one or two a week.

Review department goals and objections and assess progress each month.

By developing a plan for learning about her unit and her job, Sally will be better able to manage her unit even as she learns how to be a manager.

## NOTES

**1.** Elizabeth Fuseler Avery, Terry Dahlin, and Deborah A. Carver, *Staff Development: A Practical Guide,* 3rd ed. (Chicago: American Library Association, 2001).

**2.** Morey Stettner, *Skills for New Managers* (New York: McGraw-Hill, 2000), 15–27.

**3.** Avery, Dahlin, and Carver, *Staff Development,* 65.

**4.** Robert Lefton and Jerome Loeb, *Why Can't We Get Anything Done around Here?* (New York: McGraw-Hill, 2004), 100–121.

**5.** Linda Hill, *Becoming a Manager* (Boston: Harvard Business School Press, 2003), 52.

**6.** Martin Broadwell and Carol Broadwell Dietrich, *New Supervisor: How to Thrive in Your First Year as a Manager* (Cambridge, Mass.: Perseus Books, 1998), 27–29.

**7.** Edward Betoff and Frederick Harwood, *Just Promoted* (New York: McGraw-Hill, 1992), 22–23.

# 3
# Communication Skills

G ood communication skills are the key to being a successful supervisor because first and foremost, communication is about establishing and maintaining relationships. As a supervisor you are responsible for building your team, establishing a good working relationship with your peers, and developing a positive relationship with your boss. Good communication skills are essential if you are going to develop these diverse relationships.

Good communication is about efficiently transmitting your message. How you communicate will set the tone for your unit. If you are abrupt and noisy you will create a stressful environment. If you are always vague and unclear in your messages, you will set a tone of secrecy and uneasiness. If you are clear in your communications, you will create a healthy environment.

At the most basic level, communication involves the sender of a message, a receiver of the message, and feedback about the transmission. (See figure 3-1.)[1] When communication is successful, information is "processed, reviewed, clarified, and revised until both the sender and receiver completely understand each other.[2]

**FIGURE 3-1 ■ Communication Model**

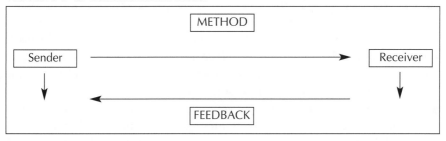

## Barriers to Communication

Unfortunately, noise in the environment can disrupt the transmission and receipt of messages. Noise can enter the communication system in the following ways.

Background chatter at meetings and side conversations can distract participants and prevent clear communication.

Interruptions can distract the speaker and cause him or her to lose track of the message.

Too much detail can inhibit effective communication. The message can be lost when too many nonessential details are included.

Irrelevant messages cause noise in the system. Messages that are not relevant to the receiver are unlikely to be remembered.

Incomprehensible jargon can also confuse the message or lead to misunderstandings.

Badly timed messages can also be unproductive. For example, asking for a detailed report on a project just as someone is leaving for the day is not going to be helpful.

Personal prejudices, stereotyping, and biases can influence how people hear a message.

Confusing or conflicting body language can disrupt communication.

The emotional state of the sender or receiver can limit their ability to send or receive information.

How can you minimize noise in your communication? Carefully planning your communication can make the difference between effective communication and noise pollution. Remember, "effective communication is primarily the speaker's responsibility."[3] Be sure you are honest, open, and clear in your communication. You don't want the receiver of your message to have to read between the lines and guess at your meaning and intent. Be alert to signals from the receiver that you are being unclear. Look for both verbal and nonverbal clues that can tell you if your message has been accurately received. Think about the purpose of your message and what you want to accomplish. Do you need someone to take action? If so, be sure you plan your message so that the action you want taken is clearly stated. Think about the recipients of your message. How much information do they need? Is this an informed audience or one with limited knowledge of your subject? Plan your communication so you link the audience and the message. Be sure the subject of your message is clear and easily identified. Obscurity and ambiguity will only create confusion. Focus and clarity will help ensure you get the results you want from your message.

## Know Your Audience

Our personalities affect how we seek and use information. In effective communication, you will want to match the form of the message to the recipient's view of the world. Carl Jung identified four types of people: thinkers who are analytical and work with facts; intuitors who deal in ideas and concepts; sensors who are action-oriented; and feelers who are ruled by emotions.[4] Each of these personality types will hear a given message differently. Sharing lots of ideas with a person who prefers facts and figures will not be very effective. Talking in terms of feelings and values to a person who wants to do something and needs action will also be ineffective. Instead, frame your ideas in data for the thinker in your unit and in action terms for the sensors. You can then effectively convey the same information to very different recipients.

## Listening

After planning your message, you can then figure out how you will listen for feedback. Active listening skills are crucial for supervisors. Obviously, you want to practice good listening skills when you are the message receiver. First, demonstrate that you are receptive to the message you are about to receive. Acknowledge the sender by nodding, injecting an occasional comment such as "yes" or "interesting" or "I see." Stay focused on the speaker and the message.

Show interest by listening carefully and attentively. Notice the speaker's emotions as well as the text of the message. Notice if the words match the emotions. If these don't match, take time to ask questions and clarify meaning until you understand how the speaker's emotional state merges with the message.

Be sure you are listening to the speaker rather than framing your response. You need to be sure you understand the message before you respond to it. If you don't listen to and clarify the message being sent before you respond, you may find yourself responding to the wrong message. You will complicate the communication process when you don't practice active listening skills.

As the receiver of a message, try not to make judgments until you have received all the information that the speaker wants to communicate. Try to listen for understanding rather than listening only for agreement. Be open to hearing other ideas even when those ideas are different from yours. If you rush to a judgment or conclusion, you may miss important details or nuances in the message. You may then respond inappropriately and may unnecessarily complicate the communication process.

One way to force yourself to pause before you respond is to silently count off a few seconds before beginning to speak. This brief silence will ensure that the speaker has completely finished his or her thoughts and is not just pausing between points.

Once it is your turn to speak, begin by asking clarifying questions. Also be sure to briefly summarize the speaker's key points before you frame your response. Only then can you be sure you have accurately heard the speaker's message.

As the sender of a message, you also want to practice active listening. Be sure you hear your receiver's response. Watch for comprehension and understanding. Ask supporting questions and provide additional information if you sense that your message is not being received. By taking time to clarify the major points of your message and taking time to actively listen to responses, you will have a better chance of creating a successful communication encounter.

## Reading

One communication challenge for supervisors is to keep up with all the written material and reading that are part of the job. Developing an efficient system for the reading of materials can make the job much easier.[5] Effective reading means developing a system for quickly scanning material, assessing the importance of the item, and locating the key messages. Keeping material from accumulating into huge piles will help keep you from becoming overwhelmed. Sort material into categories: from urgent items you need to read and act upon, to items you want to read and study in depth, to those you can declare nonessential. For unimportant items, scan them quickly and then get rid of them. Send them to be filed, throw them out, or route them as needed, but get them off your desk. Act upon or write your response to urgent items as quickly as possible. You want to resolve these issues and keep them moving. For important, in-depth items, set aside time to concentrate on these issues and read the appropriate material. Find a time during your day or week that you can set aside for in-depth study. Use that time to thoroughly read and study the important items that have reached your desk. By staying on top of your daily mail, responding to urgent items, and taking time to study the truly important material, you can be sure you are not missing key messages in your organization. You will set a good tone for your unit, since issues will not become bogged down because you didn't take time to keep up with your mail.

## Writing

As a supervisor, you will find that you need good written communication skills. You will be responsible for preparing reports, writing evaluations of your staff, developing policy statements, and communicating with your supervisors. In addition, in today's world of e-mail communication, you will also be writing messages to your staff that traditionally may have been communicated orally.

Good writing takes practice.[6] You will want to think about the message you want to convey and how you want that message to be delivered. Are you preparing a formal report to be shared with those above you in the organization? Are you sending a procedural change notification to your department? Are you communicating with groups outside of your organization? Each audience is different and has different needs. You want to be sure that your writing style is appropriate for the audience. For example, an academic-style report may be appropriate for a professional journal article, but it may not be effective for conveying information to your unit. An informal, chatty memo to your group may be fine to alert them to a minor change in policy, but this same style is not appropriate for your annual report. Be sure, then, that your style of writing fits with your audience and with the purpose of your communication.

Next, when preparing to write something, review or outline the purpose of your communication. What do you want to accomplish with your writing? Do you want to entice the public to a program or convey a policy change? Both actions are important but have very different purposes.

Third, consider the message you want to relay. What are the facts you want to get across to others? What are the key points you want to be sure your audience recognizes in your writing?

Once you have identified your audience, sufficiently outlined your purpose, and decided your main message, you are ready to begin drafting your piece. Notice the word "draft." Writing requires effort and editing. It is rare that a person can sit down and compose a memo or a report without needing to make changes and edit the document. Think about the order in which you convey the information. Your primary and important points should appear first. The reader should not have to guess at what you want someone to remember. Put the most important message first. Then add in your next most important items and so on, until you have included all the points you wish to make. Finally, write a concluding paragraph or section to summarize your key points and close your piece.

Now comes the hard part in writing. You need to review your work and edit the piece to make it as clear as possible. Eliminate any extraneous and unnecessary words. Do not use five words if three will do. Use active sentence structures to maintain clarity.

Next, check for grammar. Do all your nouns and verbs agree with each other? Have you started a paragraph each time you have a new thought or idea to express? Do you have long sentences that cannot be easily understood? Look at how you can shorten, review, and revise your work to increase clarity and understanding while still conveying all the points that you wish to make.

One helpful hint is to read your writing out loud. How does it sound? Do the words flow easily? Are the ideas clear? Reading your work out loud can help you catch grammatical errors as well as noting when you have used more words than you need.

Good written communication is a core skill for supervisors. Taking your time and reviewing your work before you distribute it will help you become an effective writer.

## E-Mail

Dangers in the world of communication include the misuse of and mistakes made through e-mail communication.[7] It is too easy, sometimes, to think you can just sit down and compose an e-mail and fire it off without review. Poorly written e-mail messages can be as dangerous for a supervisor as a poorly written report. With e-mail, as with all communication, be sure you practice good etiquette. Be careful with your use of abbreviations. For example, not everyone knows all the instant messaging abbreviations that dominate some e-mails. Be sure you explain the abbreviations you do include.

Be thoughtful about when you use e-mail. It makes very little sense to send someone an e-mail when you are sitting next to the person and can simply turn and talk to them. E-mail should not be used as a way to avoid oral communication. You should also be careful about who you send e-mails to and how you reply to messages sent to you. Do not copy everyone imaginable on an e-mail unless the information is truly needed by everyone in the organization or group. Do not reply to everyone on a discussion list message if you are sending a private reply to the sender. Not everyone on the list wants to know about your lunch plans. Keep your business e-mails business-oriented and do not confuse business and social communication.

One other trap to avoid with e-mail is the tendency to send out an e-mail reply when you are upset or angry. That is not the time to be sending messages, even to close friends, as the message could be forwarded to others. E-mail is not a secure communication channel. Rather, treat it as you would a postcard and assume everyone around will be able to see the message.

E-mail can be very effective, though, when used correctly. It can help you inform everyone in a group at the same time about a change. It can also help you document that you have relayed needed information to your group. It can help you send updates and non-time-sensitive information to a large number of people.

As a supervisor, think about what you want to communicate with your writing and then pick the best way to get your ideas across to your audience. Whether you are composing an e-mail, developing a list of bullet points, or writing a formal report, remember to think about your audience, review your purpose, and then outline your message. And finally, edit, edit, edit. A well-written and edited e-mail can help you send the kind of message you want to send to your group. A poorly written or repetitive report can just as easily hurt you. Communicating well is an art. Take time as a supervisor to practice the art of good writing each time you write.

## Your Reputation Affects Communication

As a supervisor, you will find that your "reputation, credibility, and intention" help determine how effective you can be as a communicator.[8] If you are viewed as an honest, straightforward supervisor who can be trusted, people are more likely to accept your communication at face value. They will not look for hidden meanings and devious messages. Rather, they will be open to communication from you and will try to understand what you are trying to say. If people see you as a supervisor who hides information, they will be more suspicious of communication from you. They will be more likely to look for hidden meanings and hidden agendas. Even when you are being open and honest, the staff may be leery of your communication and may be cautious in accepting information from you. As a supervisor, your actions will speak louder than your words, to quote an old cliché. In communication, as in other areas of management, you will be successful if you think about what you want to accomplish, work with your staff to be clear about your intentions, and be open to communicating and receiving information.

## Conclusion

*General communication strategies.* Good communication skills take practice to develop. Be sure you take time to learn to speak clearly, listen attentively, and respond appropriately.

*Oral communication.* Plan your communication carefully. Know what the key points are that you wish to convey. Limit how many points you want to make at any given time to the amount of information people can absorb. Providing more information than anyone can possibly comprehend in one session is not going to help you communicate your ideas.

Speak clearly and distinctly. Pause frequently and ask for questions to be sure your listeners are following your points.

Summarize your key points or actions to be taken to be sure your listeners remember the points you want to convey.

Practice active listening skills by paying attention to the speaker, clarifying his or her message before you speak, and taking time to be sure the speaker has finished before you begin to respond.

*Written communication.* If you are unsure about your writing skills, then take time to learn to write by writing. Practice writing every day. Read other people's reports and analyze the writing style. What aspects of the report are clear to you? Are there sections that don't make sense? By analyzing other people's writing, you can begin to identify what makes writing successful and what does not.

As you practice writing, employ the following rules to help simplify your writing style.[9]

1. Talk about it first. Know what you want to say before you start to write.
2. Talk to the reader on paper. Pretend the recipient of your letter is sitting across the table from you. Write your report or letter as if you were talking to this person.
3. Write to express, not impress. Write for understanding. Don't use long sentences when shorter sentences will do. Don't use so many big words that your audience cannot follow your meaning.
4. Short is better. Write enough to be clear and then stop.
5. Say it first and last. Put your purpose in your first sentence and summarize it in your last sentence.
6. Read for meaning, not glory. Reread your writing from the reader's point of view. Be sure your audience will understand your message, rather than worrying about how to make yourself look good.
7. Don't strive for perfection. There is no such thing as the perfect report. Once your piece is understandable and well organized, let it go. You have other things to do besides reediting every single document you produce.

Good communication skills come with practice. This is not a time to be lazy about learning and improving your skills. Good communication skills help you create positive working relationships with your staff, your peers, and your supervisor.

## NOTES

1. The figure is from Joan Giesecke, *Practical Strategies for Library Managers* (Chicago: American Library Association, 2001), 78.
2. William A. Salmon, *The New Supervisor's Survival Manual* (New York: AMACOM, 1999), 93.
3. Ibid., 97.
4. Arthur Young, *Manager's Handbook* (New York: Crown, 1986), 135.
5. Ibid., 138.
6. Ibid., 136–37.
7. Gary McClain and Deborah S. Romaine, *The Everything Managing People Book* (Avon, Mass.: Adams Media, 2002), 165–66.
8. Salmon, *New Supervisor's Survival Manual*, 97.
9. Young, *Manager's Handbook*, 143; and McClain and Romaine, *Everything Managing People Book*, 164–65.

# 4

# Work Climate
# and the Art
# of Motivation

A s a supervisor, you are primarily responsible for the climate in your unit. You may not realize that you have great influence over how your staff will view the unit and the organization. If you are positive and inclusive in your approach, you can create an environment where staff feel the organization cares about them. If you see the organization in "us vs. them" terms, your unit will see enemies throughout the organization. If you are passionate about the mission of the organization, you can create an atmosphere of excitement that keeps your unit motivated even in tough times.

One challenge you face in creating a good climate, though, is to recognize what kind of environment exists in your unit and organization and learn how to improve the environment if it is not as positive as you would like it to be. There are many ways to describe organizational climates. In this chapter we will look at two approaches to describe the climate in your unit, as well as ways to improve that climate.

## Character of the Organization

One way to describe the climate in your organization is to look at the organization's character. How can you describe an organization in terms of character? William Bridges, in his book *The Character of Organizations,* presents a system for using the Myers-Briggs Type Indicator system as a way to look at the character of an organization and the type of climate that character type creates.[1] His system gives supervisors a different way to think about the unit or organization and about how to develop the unit to be successful.

To follow Bridge's views, it helps to understand how the Myers-Briggs Type Indicator (MBTI) system works for individuals. "The Myers-Briggs Type Indicator is a four-letter personality-type designator created by Katharine C. Briggs and Isabel Briggs Myers in the 1940s from the theories of Carl Jung. The MBTI examines four aspects of our personalities and uses these to categorize sixteen possible personality types . . . The four scales, noted below, describe how people focus their attention, gather information, make decisions, and generally deal with the world."[2] These four scales are then used to create the sixteen temperament types: ENFJ, INFJ, ENTJ, INTJ, and so on.

*Focusing Attention*

> E *(extroversion)*—relates more to the outer world of people

> I *(introversion)*—relates more to the inner world of ideas

*Gathering Information*

> S *(sensing)*—works with facts

> N *(intuition)*—looks for possibilities and relationships

*Decision-Making*

> T *(thinking)*—decisions based on impersonal analysis and logic

> F *(feelings)*—decisions based on personal values

*Lifestyle*

> J *(judging)*—prefers a planned, orderly life

> P *(perceiving)*—prefers a flexible, spontaneous, open life

In the workplace, the sixteen personality types provide clues to how people will likely relate to work groups, decision-making, and problem-solving activities. Understanding these relationships can help supervisors decipher the behavior of the staff.

William Bridges has taken the four broad categories behind the MBTI and created a way to look at the overall character of an organization or unit. He looks at the organization's approach to its customers, how the organization gathers information, how it makes decisions, and how quickly the organization takes action. These four categories create a vocabulary for talking about the organization or unit.[3]

### Focus or Orientation of the Unit

*Extroversion*—outward-looking organizations that look to the market to determine what direction to take

*Introversion*—inward-looking organizations that look to their own technical abilities and leaders' ideas to solve problems and set directions

### Gathering Information

*Sensing*—look at facts, current realities, details of a situation

*Intuitive*—look at the big picture rather than the details

### Decision-Making

*Thinking*—impersonal decision-making, based on principles

*Feeling*—more value-driven decision-making, with a personal component

### Dealing with the World

*Judging*—tend to make decisions quickly

*Perceiving*—tend to keep options open

Each of these characteristics will yield different climates and different ways of operating in an organization. Understanding the different orientations and approaches that work in the organization can help you build a successful unit.

How can you determine the character of your organization? Bridges includes a survey instrument in his book that you and your unit can take.[4] The results of the survey will help you identify the major characteristics of your organization. Once you have taken the survey, you will want to discuss the results with your unit. You should decide how well the results describe what you already know about the organization. You can also use these discussions as opportunities to talk about how you want to function as a unit, what strengths you want to highlight, and what challenges you face as a group working within the larger organization. As a supervisor, you may find that the conversations about the organization are more important than the results of the survey. By discussing how you want to operate as a unit, you will be better able to build a working climate that is successful for the unit and the organization.

How else can you use these ideas to your advantage? In addition to using the survey results as a way to begin a conversation about the unit, you can also use Bridge's approach to help you create successful proposals that are likely to be implemented. By knowing how to bring about change, you can create a working environment that is geared to success. For example, if you and your unit wish to implement a new chat reference service or other new service, you will want to tailor your unit's proposal to match the characteristics of the organization. If your organization is basically an extroverted one that looks outward for ideas, then you will want to survey organizations that already have implemented the new reference service and describe their experiences in your proposal. If your organization is more introverted and inward-looking for advice, then you may want to ask the reference service experts in your organization to review your unit's proposal and help tailor your ideas to match the organization.

If your organization is more comfortable with facts and details, then be sure to include relevant facts and details in your proposal. For a chat reference service, include an analysis of the software used for the service, describe how reference shifts might be scheduled, and include details on the resources needed to implement the service. On the other hand, if your organization concentrates on the big-picture idea, emphasize how chat reference fits into the overall service delivery program. Describe how the new service will enhance the work of the organization. While you still need to include the details on the software to be used and how you propose to incorporate the new service into your existing structure, you will want to be more succinct and less detail-oriented in an intuitive organization than in a sensing organization.

By understanding the overall character of the organization, you can help your unit be sure that the work it does is presented in ways that will be successful in the organization. Your unit's ideas will be more likely to succeed. Your unit will be better able to contribute positively to the work of the organization. Members of your unit are less likely to become disillusioned with the organization when they can see their ideas having an impact on their work. Then you will have created a positive successful climate for your unit.

## Creating an Inclusive, Positive Climate

Another way to look at the organizational climate is to determine how inclusive that climate is for the diverse individuals in your unit. In an inclusive environment, differences among staff are recognized as strengths that you can build on in the organization. Blending and integrating those strengths will create a positive working environment where staff are inspired to do their best work.

You can build an inclusive environment by building trust among the members of your unit, treating everyone with respect, and promoting good communication.

*Trust.* This develops when staff feel they are treated fairly and as individuals. In a unit with a high level of trust, rewards are the result of effort, not favoritism. Employees must know that if they perform at the required level, you will follow through with a reward that they value.[5] Staff must feel that their views are appreciated and that their input is gathered and used. Office politics are kept to a minimum. Decision-making is transparent, and staff can see the connection between input, decision-making, and results.

*Respect.* This is another key element in creating a positive working environment. Again, when staff feel they are recognized as individuals, when their ideas are taken seriously, and when they feel their contributions are important, they will feel they are respected. If staff feel they are being treated as interchangeable parts, they may feel taken for granted and will not see the workplace as a positive environment.

*Communication.* Enough cannot be said about how important good communication is for creating a positive working environment. Good communication is a two-way process. In a positive environment, staff feel they are aware of what is going on in the unit and organization. They also feel that their input is sought and used in making the unit a success. Feeling "in the know" is a major motivator to many staff and helps them understand how they can best contribute to the unit and organization. Staff want to be part of a successful organization. Good communication is a key part of helping staff know how they can contribute to, participate in, and benefit from working in the unit and organization.

## Steps to Inclusion

What specifically can you as a supervisor do to create a positive, inclusive working climate?

First, be sure you set the right tone for the office. You must understand and accept diversity in the unit and accept the diverse contributions each individual makes to the unit. You need to be sure you are not being disrespectful to staff members and that you don't tolerate disrespectful behavior from others. For example, do not tolerate inappropriate jokes or humor. Caution staff who make inappropriate remarks about others that they must stop. If the behavior does not stop, you need to take appropriate disciplinary actions. Ignoring inappropriate behavior will create a negative environment for your unit and could result in legal action.

You need to share information with everyone in the unit, and be sure individuals are not left out of the communication loop. You need to ask for input and use that input or explain why you cannot use the input you received. In other words, make it clear to staff how you made a decision and how you used their ideas.

You also need to give credit to others for their work and ideas. You will quickly lose your staff's trust and respect if you take credit for and are rewarded for their ideas.

You need to practice listening to your staff. One of the hardest things to do as a supervisor is to really listen to ideas that are counter to what you believe and to try to find positive aspects in ideas that may not fit with your view of the unit. Even though it may be difficult to examine others' ideas, it is important to keep an open mind and explore alternative opinions. By doing so, you will form a broader view of an issue, explore new approaches, and expand your own understanding of an issue. By carefully listening to others and exploring views that don't match your own, you will help your staff members realize their ideas are valued, and therefore that they are valued as individuals and as part of the unit. For example, in our scenario of implementing a new chat reference service, as you ask your staff for ideas, keep track of the many viewpoints expressed. Then summarize those ideas for the unit to let staff know that you heard and considered their ideas. Staff can express different viewpoints on scheduling desk shifts, for instance, from how long a shift should be to how many shifts each person should work. By sharing the diversity of viewpoints, the staff will know that they have been heard and will realize that there are many ways to set up the service. Understanding different points of view will make it more likely that staff will understand why all ideas cannot be implemented.

When you can create an environment where staff are proud of what they do and feel a part of the mission of the organization, you will have the foundation for a very productive unit that can achieve excellence.

## Individual Motivation

Once you have looked at the overall climate of your unit and at how you can make that climate as positive as possible, you will want to look at how to inspire each staff member to do the best he or she can do. As a supervisor, you are responsible for creating an environment where employees are motivated to do their best work. To succeed in creating a good working environment, you need to know what motivates your staff and how you can help them to want to be productive.

Let us begin with a definition of the word "motivation." "Motivation" can be defined as giving someone an incentive to act or giving someone a reason to do something. Motivation also involves creating a feeling of enthusiasm or interest that makes someone want to do something. So the supervisor does not motivate someone, but rather creates an incentive for action. Motivation itself is self-directed. Either a staff member will want to accomplish a task or he will not. As a supervisor you want to create the best incentives you can to encourage staff to accomplish the work that needs to be done.

## Theories of Motivation

What makes people want to act? Management theorists began to address this issue in the 1950s with the human relations school of management thought. Theorists looked at individual behavior and developed theories to explain why people act in certain ways. These theories identify for supervisors what factors they need to consider in creating a motivating work climate.

Before turning to the behavioral theorists, let's review the work of Douglas McGregor and his view of management styles and motivation.[6] McGregor defined two basic approaches to management, known as Theory X and Theory Y. In Theory X, managers believe that most people do not want to work. Therefore, in order to have a productive workplace, supervisors must carefully monitor the work of the employees. Supervisors create detailed rules and procedures for staff to follow so that there is no uncertainty about what is expected or how the work is to be performed. Supervisors assume staff are lazy and will put forth the least amount of effort to get by. These supervisors create an environment that does not foster creativity, is very rule-bound, and in which staff have little or no say in how the work is performed. In Theory X, the motivating factor for staff is a paycheck.

By contrast, Theory Y managers believe that people want to do a good job. They want to create a nurturing environment where staff can be creative and contribute to the organization. Employees in Theory Y want to be useful and productive. Their motivation is the reward of a job well done.

These two views of staff motivation create two very different workplaces. In Theory X, rules and procedures are crucial, and following the rules is the key to success. In Theory Y, staff involvement in the organization and participation in decision-making lead to a productive environment. Theories X and Y illustrate how the principles of motivation that we follow affect the types of workplaces we create.

Two other major theorists in motivation are Abraham Maslow and Frederick Herzberg. Maslow looked at human behavior and theorized that people are driven by a hierarchy of needs.[7] First, people want to satisfy their need for food and shelter. Next, they will look for safety and security. Once these basic needs are fulfilled, people will try to satisfy their need for social affiliation or belonging to a group. Next, people look to fulfill their needs for self-esteem and to feel important and accepted as individuals. Finally, people have a need for self-actualization where they seek continued growth and development. In Maslow's theory, people do not have to completely satisfy one need before moving on to the next. They may work on more than one need at a time. Still, unless the basic needs are fulfilled at a minimal level, people will not be thinking about higher-level needs such as group affiliation and individual accomplishment. For a supervisor, then, if staff cannot make ends meet on the salary they receive, they are first going to be motivated to find additional sources of income. Either they will change jobs or they will find a second job to provide adequate income to meet their needs for food, shelter, and safety. Providing training so a person can learn about himself or herself as an individual will not be effective if the person cannot meet his or her basic needs. Maslow helps you as a manager to recognize that the basic resources must be in place before managers can move on to meeting higher-level needs.

Frederick Herzberg took a different approach to motivation. He theorized that there are two basic sets of motivators: positive motivators that are known as "satisfiers," and negative motivators that are known as "dissatisfiers." Positive motivators include such things as recognition, the work itself, increasing levels of responsibility, and advancement opportunities. Negative motivators are factors such as salaries, policies, types of supervision, and working conditions. These negative factors will lead to poor motivation but they do not lead to positive actions. That is, these factors may make people leave an organization but they will not necessarily keep someone working in your organization.

While theories of motivation are useful and can help you as a supervisor understand why one way of motivating staff will not work for everyone, the theories do not necessarily offer practical suggestions for how to create an environment where staff are motivated to do their best. For this, we turn to the Gallup Organization.

A third theory on motivation has been developed by the Gallup Organization and reported in the book *First, Break All the Rules*.[8] Gallup surveyed over one million individuals to identify those factors that separate organizations that are excellent performers from those that are only good.[9] Gallup found that four factors can be used by managers to determine how to create an environment that is motivating to employees. These factors are:

1. Basic resources to do the job
2. Individual needs
3. Social needs
4. Growth opportunities

Gallup isolated twelve questions that can be used to measure how well individuals believe the organization is meeting their needs. These twelve questions can then be used to distinguish those environments that lead to high performance from those that do not.

The questions are rated on a scale from 1 to 5, where 5 is "strongly agree" and 1 is "strongly disagree." In excellent organizations, employees will answer "five" to all of the questions. The twelve questions are:[10]

1. I know what is expected from me at work.
2. I have the equipment and materials I need.
3. I have the opportunity to do what I do best each day.
4. Someone at work cares about me as a person.
5. In the last seven days, I have received praise for doing good work.
6. Someone at work encourages my development.
7. The mission or purpose of the organization makes me feel my job is important.
8. My fellow employees are committed to doing quality work.
9. At work, my opinion seems to count.
10. I have a best friend at work.
11. In the last six months, someone has talked to me about my progress.

12. In the last year, I have had the opportunity at work to learn and to grow.

These questions identify factors that are similar to Maslow's hierarchy of needs. However, the order of the questions is slightly different. According to Gallup, employees first want to know what they can get from the organization. The first two questions indicate if employees' basic needs are being met. They are the organizational equivalent to safety and security needs.

Next, employees want to know what they can give to the organization, and questions 3 through 6 look at these factors. These are equivalent to Maslow's individual needs.

Third, employees will want to figure out if they belong in the organization, and questions 7 through 10 examine this issue. Here is where we find Maslow's social needs.

Finally, employees want to know if they can grow in the position, and the last two questions look at this point. Here is Maslow's self-actualization need. Gallup has found that by reversing Maslow's individual and social needs, they are better able to identify excellence in the organization. The motivational theories of Maslow, Herzberg, and the Gallup Organization are compared in figure 4-1.

**FIGURE 4-1** ■ **Theories of Motivation**

| Maslow's Hierarchy of Needs | Herzberg's Concept | Organizational Focus | Gallup's Questions Hierarchy | Organizational Focus |
|---|---|---|---|---|
| Safety and security | Dissatisfiers | Basic requirements | Expectations and resources (Q 1-2) | Basic requirements |
| Social needs | Satisfiers | Contribute to the organization | Individual and self-esteem (Q 3-6) | Individual success |
| Individual needs | Satisfiers | Individual success | Unit focus (Q 7-10) | Contribute to the organization |
| Self-actualization | Satisfiers | Growth | Growth (Q 11-12) | Growth |

## Motivational Factors and the Workplace

Gallup's questions provide a very practical way for managers to look at the environment they are creating in the workplace and examine what they need to do to move their unit to excellence.

### Clarifying Expectations and Providing Resources

Managers should first be sure that they have been clear about their expectations. Have you met with each of the employees and reviewed the expectations for their positions? Are these expectations included in job descriptions and performance evaluations? Employees should not have to guess what is expected of them. The supervisor should be able to clarify this information for each position.

Supervisors are also responsible for ensuring that employees have the resources they need to do their jobs. Staff find it very hard to feel motivated when basic equipment and supplies are not available. Employees with inadequate equipment will underperform and will lose interest in the organization. No matter how many incentives a manager creates for employees, if those employees are scrambling to find supplies and resources, they will not be spending time improving their performance.

### Identifying Individual Needs

Once the basics are in place, supervisors should talk to each employee about what they feel they do best and how that can be a part of their position or tasks. If someone's talents do not fit the job very well, they may be in the wrong position. While they may be a good performer, they will not achieve excellence if they cannot do what they do best. Employees also want to know that someone cares about them and that they receive recognition for their work. Acknowledging good performance, encouraging staff, and letting staff know you are concerned about them as individuals will go a long way to creating a motivating environment.

As you discuss each person's individual talents and ambitions, you will want to identify specific factors that help the person feel motivated to do a good job. Standard motivators include the following: a sense of achievement, a sense of power, a sense of belonging, and a sense of independence. As you talk to your staff, find out which of these needs are most important to them.[11]

To determine if a person is motivated by achievement, see if the person is goal-driven. Does the person like to work on projects? Is learning new skills important to him or her? If so, the person is likely to be looking for ways to be productive and reach new goals. Give this person new challenges. Include both short-term and long-term goals so the person can see that he or she is accomplishing tasks as a project develops.

A person who likes to exert influence and attract attention is likely to be motivated by feeling in control and feeling powerful. These staff members can be a challenge when they seek center stage and try to dominate conversations. Try to enable these staffers to contribute positively to the organization by helping them become in-house experts. Channel their energy into projects where they can express their opinions and be seen as important members of the group.

For staff who need to feel a sense of belonging, you will want to be sure they have numerous opportunities to interact with colleagues. These employees do not necessarily work well alone. Instead, find projects for them that require a group effort. These staff may also be the social organizers for the unit. Let them plan group events, staff luncheons, and other social opportunities. They will enjoy the opportunity to work with others and provide a positive social environment for the unit.

To determine if a person is motivated by independence, see if he or she questions procedures and policies that limit the individual's ability to decide how to carry out a task. You will want to be careful not to micromanage these staff. Instead, find ways they can determine their own path to achieving agreed-upon results. Of course, you will want to guard against giving these employees so much freedom that they don't follow important rules, ignore legal requirements, or refuse to work cooperatively with others.

### *Contributing to the Organization*

After examining how to meet individual needs, it is time to look at how each person can contribute to the organization. Help employees see how the mission of the organization relates to their individual tasks. Talk to people about how they make a difference. Explain to the staff or students who shelve books how they make it possible for fellow patrons or students to more easily find materials when they take time to shelve materials correctly. Show cataloging staff how the work they do makes it possible for patrons to more easily identify needed materials. Each job in the organization is important, and as supervisors you should be able to show how each position helps the organization reach its goals.

Supervisors should also be sure they are listening to staff and asking for input as appropriate. Staff will often have the best ideas on how to improve workflow and work procedures. As supervisors, we cannot be afraid to learn from our employees. Listening to staff is also a way that a supervisor can show respect for the employees. Reading or answering e-mail while listening to staff ideas will signal to the person that you do not care. When staff feel that you don't care about them as individuals, they will be less motivated to contribute to the organization.

### Growing in the Job

Finally, help people grow in their jobs. Staff do want to learn and to be challenged to improve. Motivated staff will seek out opportunities to try new things, enhance their own skills, and improve in their positions. As a supervisor, you can encourage such activities and reward people for their successes. Supervisors should talk to their staff about the progress they are making. Gallup has found that having a progress conversation at least once every six months will help staff know how they are doing. These people will stay motivated to excel.

When you have created a positive working climate, you will have a motivated staff that are inspired to do their best. Creating that climate will take work, though, as you learn how to successfully address the needs of the individuals in your unit while understanding the overall organizational environment. When you can match individual needs with organizational goals you will have a motivated staff. When you ignore individual differences and try to impose one supervisory approach on all your employees, you will leave some of your staff unmotivated and uninspired. Although it takes time to find the right combination of strategies for each person, the time will be well spent, as you will be rewarded with a well-functioning unit. You will have staff who want to work and who want to make the unit successful.

## Conclusion

Motivation comes from within individuals. You cannot motivate someone to work. You can, however, create an environment where staff are self-motivated to succeed.

Begin by analyzing the overall climate and character of your organization. Determine what strategies will be most successful within that overall climate.

Once you understand the overall climate of the organization, analyze the climate in your unit. Look for ways to create an inclusive climate that capitalizes on each person's strengths.

Determine the best way to create a motivating climate for each member of your staff. Talk to your staff about their needs. Adjust your style to address the needs of each person. Of course, you need to be sure that you are working within the overall character of the organization.

Regardless of which motivational theory you follow or which set of advice you prefer, you will be most successful when you truly listen to your staff, understand each person's needs, and match each person's needs with the tasks and projects within the unit.

## NOTES

**1.** William Bridges, *The Character of Organizations* (Palo Alto, Calif.: Consulting Psychologists, 1992), 2.

**2.** Kent Hendrickson and Joan Giesecke, "Myers-Briggs Type Indicator Profile and the Organization," *Library Administration and Management* 8, no. 4 (fall 1994): 218–19.

**3.** Bridges, *Character of Organizations,* 2–3.

**4.** Ibid., 115–19.

**5.** Patricia Buhler, *Alpha Teach Yourself Management Skills in 24 Hours* (Indianapolis, Ind.: Alpha Books, 2001), 166.

**6.** Ibid., 162–63.

**7.** Joan Giesecke, *Practical Strategies for Library Managers* (Chicago: American Library Association, 2001), 44–46.

**8.** Marcus Buckingham and Curt Coffman, *First, Break All the Rules* (New York: Simon and Schuster, 1999).

**9.** Ibid., 11.

**10.** Ibid., 43–45.

**11.** Morey Stettner, *Skills for New Managers* (New York: McGraw-Hill, 2000), 74.

# 5
# Teamwork and Group Dynamics

**M**anaging teams is part of the new challenge for today's managers. Interdivisional teams, horizontal work groups, and a variety of collaborative arrangements are replacing many of the traditional functional and hierarchical structures in our organizations. Managers today must manage interdependent groups and create a culture of cooperation in the midst of older management structures that emphasize and reward individual effort over group effort. How can managers bring these opposing processes together to create effective working groups?

## What Is a Team?

One of the first problems in determining how to manage groups is to figure out what type of working group or team environment exists or is desired in the organization. The word "team" is used to describe everything from tightly knit, interdependent working groups to loosely structured gatherings of individuals who barely work together. A "team" can be a unit or department, a group of managers, a two-person pairing such as a partnership, or the whole organization. Sometimes it seems that organizations have created teams simply by taking the departmental structure and renaming the departments as teams without making any changes in how the group functions or is managed.

Even in sports, it is difficult to identify a single type of team. For example, a football team is a highly structured group with defined roles. Players come to each other's aid only as prescribed by the structure and rules of the game. That is, the quarterback of the football team is not going to be on the field with the defense, no matter how badly the defense is playing. Nonetheless the group plays as a team, with individual roles subordinated to the team as a whole. Contrast this tightly knit, hierarchical approach with a golf team, where individual performance is most important and there is little interdependence among the players. Baseball falls somewhere between these two types of teams, with players functioning independently in their individual positions, but needing to interact in prescribed ways on the field if they are to win the game. In organizations, the independent golf team approach where each person does their own job with little interaction with others is becoming obsolete. Rather, organizations are finding that teams or work groups that require collaboration, commitment, and trust are more common and more productive than independent groups. But given this wide range of types of teams, what does the word "team" really mean in the workplace?

Jon Katzenbach and Douglas Smith, in their book *The Wisdom of Teams,* provide a succinct definition of a team. They describe a true working team as "a small number of people with complementary skills who are committed to a common purpose, performance goals, and approach for which they hold themselves mutually accountable."[1]

The key concepts in this definition help define the requirements for a true working team. To be a team, the group needs to be small enough that people can interact regularly and effectively. Team members get to know each other, build working relationships, and meet regularly. When the group gets too big—more than twenty-five people—it becomes more difficult to meet, to interact, and to work together. In larger groups, subgroups may form and the whole unit no longer functions as a coordinated team. Rather, the larger group may follow team values, but not have the interactions that characterize effective teams.

Team members possess complementary skills, rather than identical skills. Each team member brings unique skills to the group so that the group as a whole has all the proficiencies needed to accomplish assigned tasks. Having a group of people all with the same skills doing the same task is a working unit rather than a team. A group of online cataloging staff who all do the same task of cataloging materials using records on OCLC is a working unit, not a team. Each person's performance is independent of the others in the group. While group goals can be developed, the individual employees can set their own pace and can do much of their work without consulting others as long as standards and expectations are clear. Here team values may be useful, but the group is not a true team.

The overall picture of a team is an interdependent group with a common goal or purpose. The team members are working toward and accept an agreed-upon purpose or set of goals. Individuals do not set their own goals; instead, group goals define the course for the team. In football, for example, the defense may have team goals on how many turnovers they want to cause in a game. In the library, the interlibrary loan staff may set goals on turnaround time and the fill rate for requests. To achieve these goals, the group members must work together. Goals cannot be achieved by individual effort alone.

Team members also agree on how the work will be done. Internal procedures are explored and agreed upon by the team. Problem-solving and decision-making processes are clear and understood by all members of the team. Team members also understand that each person contributes to the work of the whole. The amount of work that is done is equitably distributed, with each team member contributing to the best of their ability. Unlike groups where some people may contribute very little but get credit for the work of the whole, in a true team all team members agree to participate to make the team a success.

This brings us to shared accountability, which is a key factor in a true team. Team members agree to take responsibility for their own work and the work of the team. They help each other out as needed. They encourage each other to do the best each one can for the team. Individual responsibility gives way to group responsibility and mutual respect and support.

## Characteristics of Effective Teams

If the group you are managing fits the definition of a true work team, then your next step as a manager is to understand the characteristics of an effective team, because not all teams function well. Teams can be as dysfunctional as any unit or department in any management style. Successful teams have the following characteristics:[2]

Team members understand and support the organization's vision and goals.

Teams share a set of values about quality service.

Teams try to improve work processes and operations.

Team members discuss and agree as to how decisions will be made, how communication will occur, and how the group will be managed.

Team members listen to each other, respect each other, and trust each other.

Assignments and responsibilities are clear. Roles are clear and understood.

Teams effectively manage external policies, processes, and politics.

Teams set results-oriented goals.

Teamwork enhances the ability of the team members to work together, i.e., team members continue to learn how to work together more effectively. Team members are satisfied to work together.

Teams adapt to changing environments, anticipate each other's moves, and learn to regenerate themselves as they work together.

Successful teams have committed, focused leaders who facilitate group success.

Teamwork, then, can be described as a "frame of mind, a belief, and a commitment, not just a program."[3] In a team, group goals are more important than individual goals. Team members believe in the value of group process and work to ensure that processes complement productivity. Decision-making systems, communication systems, and work processes are equally important to meeting the team's goals. Productivity is not sacrificed to ensure good group interactions, nor are good group interaction skills ignored in order to maintain or improve productivity. A cohesive approach that brings team values together with team productivity is crucial if one is to create a true team.

## How Can You Recognize a True Team?

An example from an interlibrary loan unit might illustrate some of the differences between a work group and a team. Imagine an interlibrary loan unit with five staff members and one manager. Two of the staffers work on lending requests, two work on borrowing requests, and one serves as a reception desk attendant. A problem arises with the workflow between a branch library and the main library for obtaining books requested by other libraries in a timely manner. In a work group, the lending staff might discuss the problem with the unit supervisor and generate possible solutions. The unit supervisor might set up a meeting with branch and interlibrary loan staff. Then the group discusses the problem and proposes solutions. The supervisor decides which solution to implement. While the various staff involved provide input and discuss the issues, they are not empowered to make a decision and implement that decision.

In a team environment, the five interlibrary loan staff members and the supervisor would discuss the problem with the branch staff. The group as a whole would generate options, assess possibilities, and decide the best way to improve workflow to meet agreed-upon goals for turnaround time. The lending and borrowing staffs would both participate in the discussion, because changes in work routines can potentially impact the unit in any number of ways. By working together, the unit and branch staff will likely find solutions that work for all units involved. The group is not only responsible for implementing the changes, but is also accountable for the success of those changes.

Agreed-upon goals, responsibility, and shared accountability are all part of a true team environment. This still leaves the question of how to recognize a true team. What distinguishes a team from a working group? Again, we can turn to Katzenbach and Smith, who created a performance curve for teams and groups to illustrate the differences among various types of work units. They use the criteria of performance impact and team effectiveness to distinguish between the various types of units.[4]

At one end of the scale are work groups. These are probably the most common form of structure in our organizations. In these units, individual effort is the primary measurement for unit success. Members may come together to share information, insights, or ideas on how to improve the unit. However, individual performance goals are more important than joint work products. Members of the unit interact but are not dependent on each other for either their own or the unit's success.

The second type of unit can be described as a pseudo-team. Here the work of the unit lends itself to true group-based performance, but the members of the unit don't actually work together to achieve unit-wide goals. These units are not very productive because individual interests are more important to members than group success. Pseudo-teams may form when a manager or library director decides to rename work units as teams without making any changes in group interactions. The label for the group changes without any change in how the group actually functions.

The next type of group on the performance continuum is the potential team. Potential teams are those groups that are trying to improve group performance, are becoming committed to group goals, and are beginning to recognize the need for mutual respect and accountability. If you are a manager with a potential team, you can help the group achieve high productivity through team development and training. Potential teams in an organization offer managers the chance to implement change and achieve success.

Real teams, the next type on the continuum, are those units that meet the definition of a team and are reaching mutually agreed-upon goals. These groups are effective, productive, and can be successful over time.

High-performance teams are at the end of the continuum. These are groups that not only function effectively but are also deeply committed to each other's growth and success. These teams surpass goals, have high energy levels, and provide support for each other while meeting organizational goals.

The performance characteristics of these five types of groups are summarized in figure 5-1.

**FIGURE 5-1 ■ Team Performance Characteristics**

| Type of Group | Motivation to Perform | Measure of Team Success |
|---|---|---|
| Work group | Individual goals | Successful or not successful |
| Pseudo-team | Selfish interests | Not successful |
| Potential team | Organization sets group goals | Partially successful |
| Real team | Mutually agreed-upon goals | Successful |
| High-performance team | Surpass goals, committed to team growth | Most successful |

As a supervisor or manager in a team-based organization, you will want to move your group from a potential team to a real or a high-performance team. If you have a work group, then a team structure may not be the best way to organize your unit. Here you need to look at the purpose and organizational goals for your unit. If interdependence is not a key factor in accomplishing your goals, then a team structure may not be needed. A solid working group that shares team values and meets its performance goals may be most effective for your unit. If you have a pseudo-team, you will need to do a lot of staff development and training to change your unit from a group to a team.

## Developing Teams

Before you begin a team-building program, it is helpful to look at the context in which your unit operates because that context impacts team effectiveness. James Shank, in his book *Working in Teams,* outlines five factors that affect teams: environmental influences, goals, roles, processes, and relationships.[5] Let's look at each of these factors as they apply to our interlibrary loan unit.

*Environmental influences.* Environmental influences are the external forces that affect teamwork. They include such things as policies, reward systems, organizational structures, customers, and governmental regulations. For the interlibrary loan unit, organizational policies such as who can use the service, how the service is funded, and what hours the library is open will frame how the unit functions. Reward structures, such as how salaries are distributed or what types of awards are available, can also impact the unit. For example, if only individual effort is rewarded, it will be more difficult to convince the staff to work as a team. The lending operations staff may be less inclined to support the borrowing staff if the former's efforts are not acknowledged by the organization.

*Goals.* Agreed-upon goals are the foundation for teamwork. Goals need to be clear, specific, and shared. In interlibrary loan, goals on turnaround time, fill rate, and quantity of work to be accomplished all determine how the group will design the workflow. For example, if a goal of 24-hour turnaround time on lending requests is set and the lending staff have an unusually busy day, then in a team approach, the borrowing staff would help the lending staff to complete their work. The team as a whole takes responsibility for achieving the goal.

*Roles.* Quite simply, clarifying roles means deciding who does what. For interlibrary loan, the group needs to know who processes lending requests, who monitors OCLC requests, who oversees mail operations, and who manages the reception desk. It is also important for the group to know who the primary backup is for each task and how team members will know when their help is needed.

*Processes.* Processes are the internal procedures that determine how the team does its work. In interlibrary loan, the group decides how long to spend on difficult requests before referring them to someone else. The team also needs to decide how decisions will be made and how meetings will be run. The team members decide and agree upon which libraries will be contacted for materials and in what order, how consortium arrangements affect lending response and borrowing options, and how materials will be delivered to patrons. All these processes should be clear to all members of the team.

*Relationships.* The last factor to consider in understanding your team is the quality of the interpersonal interactions within it. Team members should develop their own guidelines on how they will interact, how difficult issues will be discussed, and how disagreements will be handled. In the interlibrary loan unit, disagreements on what steps to take to resolve a patron problem need to be addressed. The staff must develop ways to express and address different opinions and viewpoints. If they don't address these issues, team effectiveness will suffer.

To summarize, these five factors are key considerations as you design team-building programs for your group. Addressing these areas in your development program will help improve team effectiveness.

## Designing a Team-Building Program

Team-building programs can vary from a short discussion on the value of teams to a multiday retreat with a trained facilitator. How you design your program will depend on how your organization functions and how it supports staff development. Does your organization have a formal staff development program or training unit? Does it have funds you can use to hire a facilitator to help? Does the organization have trained facilitators you can consult as you think about staff development? Know what resources you can use and what support you can find before you decide on a particular program or approach.

No matter how you design staff development efforts for team-building, there are some common guidelines for success that you can follow.[6]

*Establish clear goals.* Be specific about what you want your team-building to accomplish. Do you need new goals, new standards, or a new structure? Clarifying your goals will help guide your planning.

*Get input.* Effective team-building starts by getting team members to help design the program. Involving team members in the planning will help them to "buy in" to the program. Imposing a training program on the group will be less effective.

*Model constructive behavior.* Focus on behavior and performance in the training rather than on judging opinions or positions. Staff should learn the effect that different behaviors have on the unit and how appropriate behaviors can improve team performance.

*Stay work-oriented.* It is important to avoid team-building that can become too emotional, with too much sharing of non-work-related information. Stay focused on projects and the responsibilities of the team. In interlibrary loan, training examples should be based on the processes of borrowing and lending materials and document delivery rather than on the personal lives of the team members.

*Allow time for change.* Team-building takes time. Change will happen, but it will not happen overnight. Team members need time to practice new skills, try new processes, and explore new ideas. Look for incremental progress and reward even small changes that are positive.

*Assess development.* Teams can conduct self-assessments throughout the development and training process so that the team can judge its own progress. Have the team members individually complete assessment tools and then discuss the results. Team members can use these discussions as opportunities to plan and guide future development efforts.

Assessment tools usually ask team members to rank how well the team is doing in[7]

- clarifying purpose
- clarifying expectations
- developing open communication systems
- providing mutual support
- developing conflict resolution skills
- clarifying decision-making processes
- encouraging risk-taking

- sharing leadership
- sharing feedback

*Develop realistic expectations.* Credibility and trust are easy to lose if you set expectations that cannot be met by the group. Expectations for training should address those factors that are within the group's control. For example, increasing the team's understanding of each person's role, clarifying team goals, and improving conflict resolution skills are all factors that the team can control. Training in these areas will result in team improvement.

*Utilize outside consultants.* Finally, if possible, it can be very helpful to engage an outside trainer or facilitator to assist with team development. An outside person can help facilitate communication and remain objective more easily than someone from inside the team. Bringing in an outside person can help the team see new approaches and find new ways of working together.

Following these concepts will help you design effective training for your group no matter what training methods are used.

## Team Training Plans

There are many ways to develop training plans and many methods that can be used. As a manager, you will want to match the training method to your team's needs.

Describing all the possible training options is beyond the scope of this book. You can find helpful examples of training methods in the third edition of *Staff Development: A Practical Guide,* by Elizabeth Fuseler Avery, Terry Dahlin, and Deborah Carver.[8] In their book *Just Promoted,* Edward Betoff and Frederic Harwood include a matrix you can use to evaluate the type of training that is needed and the methods that will be most successful.[9] Designing good training programs takes time, thought, and resources. Your organization's staff development experts can be very helpful to you as you develop programs to build and strengthen your team.

## When Teams Fail

What causes teams to fail? Why don't all work groups succeed as teams? The causes for failure are numerous because teams are often a paradox. Team leaders and teams must balance individual differences with collective identity, support with confrontation, and management authority with team autonomy.[10] These conflicting ideas and concepts must be brought into harmony for teams to succeed.

Numerous forces can work against team success in an organization. Some of these forces include lack of respect, selfishness, backbiting, politics, blame, and unaddressed feelings.[11] Immature approaches to the team by individual team members can defeat even the best team-building efforts.

*Lack of respect.* If team members don't have respect for each other or for the organization, it will be difficult if not impossible to turn the group into a team. It may be more productive to move people out of the group and get new members in order to build a viable team.

*Selfishness.* When staff members care more about what they can get as individuals than they do about the group, you will have problems building a team. Staff members who argue over who gets a new pencil sharpener or mouse pad are not ready for team-building. Here, as a supervisor, you need to step back and start with basic training in good group skills before you can begin team-building.

*Politics.* If organizational politics are more important than the team, you have an immature group. Again, look for training options for basic skills with which to help staff move beyond an individual focus and start thinking about the group goals.

*Blame.* If the group starts the conversation about a problem with "Who is to blame?" you have an immature group. An interlibrary loan staff, for example, that blames others for poor turnaround time instead of looking for a solution they can implement is not a well-functioning team. Blaming poor shelving, branch staff ineptitude, or poorly documented patron requests are all examples of immature group behavior.

In all these cases, the culture of the group or the group members needs to change before true team-building can begin.

## The Supervisor's Role in Teams

By now you may be wondering what your role as a manager is in the team environment. Are you a team leader, a team member, or just one of the crowd? What role do you play in this type of organizational structure? As team leader you are responsible for the following roles.[12]

*Understand and be committed to the team concept.* First, as a manager, you need to understand the team concept. If you play favorites or reward and promote individual achievement over group goals, you will undermine team efforts. If you are not committed to a team structure, you will not be effective as a team leader.

*Select team members.* As team leader you are responsible for choosing the members of your team. Look for complementary skills so you can build a group of people with the variety and depth of skills you need for success.

*Develop people skills.* As a manager, you need to recognize and acknowledge team members' skill-building efforts. Even something as simple as saying "Good job" or "That's a good effort" will support people-building skills. Recognizing that different people want different types of recognition is important too. Some people like public recognition; some prefer a personal letter. As a team leader you need to understand your team members as individuals at the same time that you promote group coordination and collaboration.

*Facilitate information flow.* Another major role for you as leader is to facilitate, support, and promote the flow of information. You bring in information from the rest of the organization. You facilitate the sharing of information about your unit with the organization. And you support the coordination of effort within the group through the sharing of information.

*Coordinate with your peers.* As team leader, you are charged with working effectively with other team leaders to advance the goals of the organization. In interlibrary loan, for example, you may be working with an acquisition unit to be sure that heavily requested items are considered for purchase. You may coordinate searching activities with a reference unit. You may work with a cataloging unit to be sure the catalog records contain enough detail for your unit to verify the ownership of a particular item. In each of these venues, you want to represent the goals and needs of your team while sharing the concerns of other units with your group.

*Pay attention to first meetings.* As team leader, you will set the tone for how the group initially interacts. If you show that you are flexible, committed to team goals, and responsive to the group, you will set a positive tone that will carry the group through its first few meetings. By sending a clear signal that you support the team as a team, you will encourage the development of good team guidelines and processes.

*Set clear rules for behavior.* Help the group establish clear ground rules as they begin to form as a team. Agreements on attendance, discussion options, confidentiality, meeting process, and so on should be established early in the process so the team can function effectively as a group while they build their skills to become a true team. Disagreements or resentments over simple items such as the time allowed for personal phone calls or the length of breaks can destroy team trust and make the group dysfunctional.

*Spend lots of time together.* As a leader you need to spend time with your team. Absentee management will not work in a team environment. Delegating work to the group and then disappearing from the unit will not work either. Team efforts require the group to work together. As team leader, you need to be a part of the group at the same time that you provide leadership and help set direction.

*Provide positive feedback and constructive advice.* As team leader, you are also responsible for providing feedback to the group. The team members need to know how they are performing as a group, how they are meeting goals, and how they are interacting. Effective leaders provide appropriate feedback and advice even as they function as part of the team. (See the team evaluation tool in figure 5-2.)[13]

*Keep goals relevant.* As team leader, you can help guide the group to ensure that its agreed-upon goals and purpose mesh well with the overall goals of the organization. If your organization values customer service, then help your interlibrary loan team to develop goals around response time, number of patron complaints, or number of patrons served. Matching unit goals to organizational goals is crucial if the team is to remain relevant to the organization.

*Create opportunities for others.* Team leaders cannot take all the desirable assignments, praise, or glory and still expect to have a successful team. Rather, true team leaders share opportunities, plum assignments, and rewards with the team. Watching staff develop into successful team members is a reward to a true team leader.

*Do real work.* Team leaders are important members of the team. While the role of team leader means that you have responsibilities outside of the team, you also have real work responsibilities inside the team. A team leader in interlibrary loan will help with lending requests or borrowing requests when needed and not just sit around while team members struggle to complete a day's set of requests.

## Conclusion

Successful teams don't happen by accident. Building successful teams involves planning and effort. As a supervisor, before you embark on a team-building effort, assess your unit's readiness to be a team. Be sure the work

FIGURE 5-2 ■ Evaluating Your Team Development

## RATING TEAM DEVELOPMENT

How do you feel about your team's progress? (*Circle rating*).

1. Team's purpose
    *I'm uncertain* ➤ 1  2  3  4  5 ◄ *I'm clear*
2. Team membership
    *I'm out* ➤ 1  2  3  4  5 ◄ *I'm in*
3. Communications
    *Very guarded* ➤ 1  2  3  4  5 ◄ *Very open*
4. Team goals
    *Set from above* ➤ 1  2  3  4  5 ◄ *Emerged through team interaction*
5. Use of team members' skills
    *Poor use* ➤ 1  2  3  4  5 ◄ *Good use*
6. Support
    *Little help for individuals* ➤ 1  2  3  4  5 ◄ *High level of support for individuals*
7. Conflict
    *Difficult issues are avoided* ➤ 1  2  3  4  5 ◄ *Problems are discussed openly and directly*
8. Influence on decisions
    *By few members* ➤ 1  2  3  4  5 ◄ *By all members*
9. Risk-taking
    *Not encouraged* ➤ 1  2  3  4  5 ◄ *Encouraged and supported*
10. Working on relationships with others
    *Little effort* ➤ 1  2  3  4  5 ◄ *High level of effort*
11. Distribution of leadership
    *Limited* ➤ 1  2  3  4  5 ◄ *Shared*
12. Useful feedback
    *Very little* ➤ 1  2  3  4  5 ◄ *Considerable*

of the unit fits well in a team environment. Evaluate the strengths of your staff and analyze the skills your unit will need to succeed as a team. Then, if the work and environment match the team concept, begin discussing the change to a team approach with your staff. Work together to develop strategies to become a successful team. By working together, your unit can move to a true team environment and will be successful in this different approach to managing the work of the group.

## NOTES

1. Jon Katzenbach and Douglas Smith, *The Wisdom of Teams* (Boston: Harvard Business School Press, 1993), 45.

2. Edward Betoff and Frederic Harwood, *Just Promoted* (New York: McGraw-Hill, 1992), 128.

3. Martin Broadwell and Carol Broadwell Dietrich, *New Supervisor: How to Thrive in Your First Year as a Manager* (Cambridge, Mass.: Perseus Books, 1998), 273.

4. Katzenbach and Smith, *The Wisdom of Teams,* 90–99.

5. James Shank, *Working in Teams* (New York: AMACOM, 1982), 19–21.

6. Betoff and Harwood, *Just Promoted,* 131–32.

7. The list is adapted with permission from Arnold Bateman, *Team Building: Developing a Productive Team* (Lincoln: University of Nebraska-Lincoln, 1990).

8. Elizabeth Fuseler Avery, Terry Dahlin, and Deborah Carver, *Staff Development: A Practical Guide,* 3rd ed. (Chicago: American Library Association, 2001), 125–46.

9. Betoff and Harwood, *Just Promoted,* 140–42.

10. Linda Hill, *Becoming a Manager* (Boston: Harvard Business School Press, 2003), 297.

11. Broadwell and Dietrich, *New Supervisor,* 268–69.

12. Katzenbach and Smith, *Wisdom of Teams,* 119–27; Broadwell and Dietrich, *New Supervisor,* 270–71.

13. The figure is adapted with permission from Arnold Bateman, *Team Building: Developing a Productive Team* (Lincoln: University of Nebraska-Lincoln, 1990).

# 6

# Inclusiveness and Diversity

*The great organization must not only accommodate the fact that each employee is different, it must capitalize on these differences.*
—Marcus Buckingham and Donald O. Clifton

## What Is Diversity?

At the most basic level, diversity is the existence and recognition of differences. These differences may be ones of ethnicity, race, nationality, gender, age, physical disabilities, or sexual orientation. Janice Joplin and Catherine Daus state, "Diversity encompasses any characteristic used to differentiate one person from others."[1] Building on this definition, managing inclusiveness and diversity means taking advantage of the diversity in the workplace to build a stronger organization. When we value diversity, we can "solve problems using multiple perspectives, relate to customers in their native language and culture, [and] improve communication."[2]

Over the next fifty years, it is anticipated that the United States will experience a sharp rate of growth in ethnic minority (nonwhite) populations.

By the year 2050, minorities will account for 50 percent of the overall U.S. population.[3] These changing demographics mean that unless the library workforce also experiences a significant increase in the hiring of minorities, librarians and library staff will increasingly be serving students, faculty, and citizens not like themselves. The recruitment and retention of a diverse workforce, while an important issue for libraries during the past few decades, is now more important than ever.

In this chapter we will discuss the benefits of a diverse workforce, the challenges it poses for supervisors, and how to recognize strengths and capitalize on differences in your employees.

## The Diverse Workforce

A library (or any organization) with a diverse workforce, with individuals willing to share new ideas based on their backgrounds and experiences, will be in a better position to meet the needs of our changing user populations. Better problem-solving and increased creativity and innovation are the results of well-managed diversity in an organization.[4] A culturally diverse library staff brings different perspectives to library work, which traditionally, at least in the United States, has had an Anglo-European cultural context. Many libraries have developed diversity plans to help guide their work in this area. Consult with your library administration to see if your library has such a plan.

As a supervisor, you have an important opportunity to help create a diverse unit, as well as one with staff members who appreciate and respect diversity. Your unit will move forward to meet the organization's goals more fully by promoting acceptance of and respect for different people, ideas, and opinions. Recognizing differences in learning styles and communication styles will enable you to work most effectively with the staff members you supervise.

## Cultural Differences

Mainstream American culture has been heavily influenced by white or Anglo cultural norms. Creating an environment that welcomes, values, and respects all members requires us to develop an understanding of cultural differences and to realize that not all members of a particular culture will exhibit the same traits or behaviors. For example, researchers have studied variations in the preferred learning styles of Native Americans, Hispanic Americans, African Americans, Asian Americans, and European Americans.

As a supervisor, you will want to consider learning style preferences when you are training new employees and when providing staff development opportunities for current staff.

## Generational Differences

In recent years the popular press has published much information about generational differences and, particularly, the factors that motivate different generations. Most current library employees belong to one of four generations: veterans, born between 1925 and 1945; baby boomers, born between 1946 and 1963; generation X, born between 1964 and 1979; and generation Y or millennials, born between 1980 and 1994. For supervisors, each group poses unique challenges. For example, veterans may be reluctant to buck the system, uncomfortable with conflict, and reluctant to disagree. Baby boomers may be overly sensitive to feedback, judgmental of those who see things differently, and like veterans, uncomfortable with conflict and reluctant to go against their peers. Since baby boomers developed much of the "system" that the veterans don't want to "buck," this leaves baby boomers and veterans together in the "we've always done it this way" camp, which can be frustrating for impatient generation Xers. Generation X employees may be inexperienced, have poor people skills, and are often cynical. Like generation Xers, millennials are also inexperienced, although for different reasons. Generation Xers have not had the chance to experience some aspects of work culture because of a lack of opportunity. Positions they may seek are still held by veterans and baby boomers who continue to work in their organizations. Millennials' lack of experience is largely due to their young age, as well as the types of childhoods that many of them have experienced. Millennials are used to close supervision of their education, their social activities, and, in fact, all aspects of their lives. They have new supervisory needs, different from those who came before them.[5]

For more information on these issues, you can consult one of the many books and articles written on this topic in the past few years. *Millennials Go to College,* by Neil Howe and William Strauss, is an excellent resource for more in-depth coverage of generational issues.[6]

## Gender Differences

Even though we have made strides in achieving gender equity, understanding gender differences without stereotyping employees is still important today. Libraries traditionally employ more females than males, although

upper-level management positions in libraries continue to include a dispro-
portionate number of males. Gender differences may account for many of
the communication issues that arise in libraries. Compounded by generational differences and cultural differences, gender differences may have
major implications for supervisors.

Men and women bring different strengths to the workplace. Gender-
based differences in approaches to communication, problem-solving, and relationships are evident in young children and continue throughout our lives.

Boys tend to play in hierarchical groups with one boy acting as leader,
giving orders, and telling others what to do. Boys play games with winners
and losers, and elaborate systems of rules. In contrast, girls play in small
social groups that are cooperative and inclusive, and their games do not
necessarily have winners and losers. Girls are more concerned with being
liked than with attaining status within the group.[7]

In the workplace, this playground behavior pattern continues.
Generally, men are more likely to be directive, to tell others what to do, to
resent interruptions, and to value the completion of tasks and goals. Women
tend to work at a steady pace, not consider interruptions as a problem,
prefer face-to-face or group interaction over written, impersonal communication, and maintain a complex set of relationships. Men seem to be more
task-focused while women are more relationship-focused.[8]

These generalizations may help you as a supervisor to understand or
interpret behavior that is different from your own. But as a manager, you
will want to be sure you are not seeing your employees as categories or
stereotypes. Use the research that helps explain differences to understand
how to adapt your style to be more effective. You want to capitalize on each
person's strengths, not discount someone based on an arbitrary category.

Imagine you are Mark, the manager of a department of six reference
librarians. You want the group to function well together, but you recognize
that much of their work is done as individuals at a reference desk and while
covering an online chat reference service. Your department has three men
and three women in it. Mark needs to be sure he resists the temptation to
ask the women to arrange all the department social events or to pitch in and
cover when someone is sick. He needs to be sure he expects the same level of
cooperation from his male employees as he does from his female employees.

Mark will also want to consider how he communicates. While he may
be very direct and directive with male colleagues, he may want to use a
more inclusive language style with his female colleagues and staff. Mark can
do a lot to promote harmony in his unit by recognizing different approaches

and styles and using those differences to bring multiple perspectives to the unit's work.

## Physical Disabilities

In your role as supervisor, you are responsible for working with your library or organization to provide a welcoming and inclusive environment for all staff, including those with physical disabilities. For staff who are deaf or hard of hearing, always face the staff member when speaking with him or her. This will help the staff members to hear as much as possible, and allow them to see lip-reading cues. Consider carefully the seating arrangement in the work area and at meetings. Provide written materials prior to meetings or presentations, so that the staff person has some time to process the information. For visually impaired staff, be sure that written documentation is clear black-on-white copy. Policies and procedures should be conveyed verbally to the employee. During meetings and presentations, be sure that seating is available to allow the staff member to hear as much as possible. When possible, tape record meetings so that the staff member can review them as needed. If mobility is an issue for a staff member, work with the employee to determine appropriate tools and work space configuration. If arm or hand mobility is limited, consider structuring job duties so that the staff member works together with another staff member for tasks that require lifting, etc. When speaking with a staff member in a wheelchair, sit down during your discussion so that you are both at the same eye level. Do not make assumptions about wheelchair users; lower-body mobility problems may be their only difficulty. In this case, they are no different than any other staff person who is seated. Look for areas where your library or organization can improve access for individuals with physical disabilities.

## Sexual Orientation

Gay, lesbian, bisexual, and transgendered (GLBT) staff members seek a safe working environment where all employees are treated with respect, regardless of their sexual orientation or identity. As supervisor, you can set the tone for your department or unit by your responses to GLBT issues. Respond to negative remarks or jokes in a way that demonstrates that you, and the library, do not tolerate this sort of disrespectful behavior. Other staff will respond to the way you handle these situations. Educate yourself about GLBT issues if you are not already familiar with them. Learn more about local resources, on campus or in your community; many campuses have GLBT offices that can provide information and assistance.

## The Importance of Recognizing Strengths

Recognizing the strengths of individual staff members can help you to channel their activities in the ways that will be most beneficial to your unit. There are a number of personality indicators or trait surveys that can help individuals to determine their areas of strength. As with all surveys or testing measures, the findings should be considered as just a small part of the package the individual brings to their position and should never be used to stereotype an employee. As Gordon Lawrence states, "We tend to stereotype those who are most different from ourselves because we understand them less well—a rule that holds true for type differences as well as cultural, racial, etc."[9] As a supervisor, it is your responsibility to ensure that, if your organization does use personality type indicators, you work with staff members in your unit to examine their own stereotypes and not impose them on their coworkers.

Two common workplace personality measures are the Myers-Briggs Type Indicator and the Gallup StrengthsFinder Profile.

### Myers-Briggs Type Indicator

The Myers-Briggs Type Indicator (MBTI) is a personality-type designator created by Katharine C. Briggs and Isabel Briggs Myers in the 1940s based on the theories of the psychologist Carl Jung. The MBTI examines four aspects of personality: attention focus, information-gathering, decision-making style, and lifestyle. It uses these factors to categorize sixteen possible personality types. The sixteen personality types provide clues to how people will likely relate to work groups, decision-making, and problem-solving activities. Understanding these relationships can help supervisors decipher the behavior of staff. In work situations, these factors can be described as follows.

#### FOCUSING ATTENTION

*Extroversion (E).* Extroverts like variety and action. They can be impatient with long slow jobs. They like having people around. They are interested in results, getting the job done, and how other people do it. Often extroverts act quickly, sometimes without thinking.

*Introversion (I)*. Introverts like quiet for concentration. They tend to be careful with details and dislike sweeping statements. They are interested in the idea behind their job. They dislike telephone intrusions and interruptions. Introverts like to think a lot before they act. They work contentedly alone.

## GATHERING INFORMATION

*Sensing (S)*. Sensing types dislike new problems unless there are standard ways to solve them. They like an established way of doing things. They work more steadily, with realistic ideas of how long it will take. Sensing types usually reach a conclusion step by step. They are patient with routine details and impatient when the details get complicated.

*Intuition (N)*. Intuitives like solving new problems. They dislike doing the same thing repeatedly. They work in bursts of energy powered by enthusiasm, with slack periods in between. Intuitives reach a conclusion quickly. They are impatient with routine details but are patient with complicated situations.

## DECISION-MAKING

*Thinking (T)*. Thinking types do not show emotion readily and are often uncomfortable dealing with people's feelings. They may hurt people's feelings without knowing it. They like analysis and putting things into logical order. Thinkers need to be treated fairly.

*Feelings (F)*. Feeling types tend to be very aware of other people and their feelings. They enjoy pleasant people, and they like harmony. Feeling types' efficiency may be badly disturbed by office feuds. They need occasional praise.

## LIFESTYLE

*Judging (J)*. Judging types work best when they can plan their work and follow the plan. They like to get things settled and finished. Sometimes judging types may decide things too quickly. They want only the essentials needed to begin their work.

*Perceivers (P)*. Perceptive types adapt well to changing situations. They do not mind leaving things open for alterations. They may have trouble making decisions. Perceivers want to know all about a new job.

In chapter 4 on motivation, the Myers-Briggs Type Indicator is used to discuss the character of an organization. For more information about the MBTI, consult the resources listed at the end of this chapter.

## StrengthsFinder Profile

The Gallup Organization, over the course of many years of surveys and research, determined that the best managers have two assumptions about their staff: each person's talents are enduring and unique, and each person's greatest room for growth is in the areas of his or her greatest strengths.[10]

The Gallup Organization found thirty-four patterns that are the most prevalent themes of human talent. The thirty-four themes are:[11]

| | | |
|---|---|---|
| achiever | developer | learner |
| activator | discipline | maximizer |
| adaptability | empathy | positivity |
| analytical | fairness | relator |
| arranger | focus | responsibility |
| belief | futuristic | restorative |
| command | harmony | self-assurance |
| communication | ideation | significance |
| competition | inclusiveness | strategic |
| connectedness | individualization | woo |
| context | input | |
| deliberative | intellection | |

These thirty-four themes are the basis of the StrengthsFinder Profile, introduced in the book *Now, Discover Your Strengths,* by Marcus Buckingham and Donald O. Clifton. The StrengthsFinder's purpose is to help individuals find those areas where they show the greatest potential for strength. For supervisors, recognizing areas of staff talent will enable you to help individual staff members to make the most of their potential. Gallup calls this "individualization."[12] By focusing on each employee's individual strengths, you can adapt the way that you work with the employee in areas such as your communication style, how you provide feedback, and how you motivate for optimal performance.[13]

Buckingham and Clifton provide suggestions for how to manage each of the different themes, or strengths, of individual staff members. Once you know the top themes for an employee, you can work together with that employee to develop his or her strengths.

## Retention

Retaining a diverse workforce is crucial. Building a culture that welcomes diverse opinions and experiences is the first step in retention. There are many ways to change an organization's culture. One way that some libraries have adopted is to become a learning organization. Learning organizations value sharing ideas throughout the organization. Members share experiences, skills, and expertise, and in doing so, build respect for all members of the organization, and promote an organizational culture and work environment of inclusiveness. This provides a strong foundation for retaining a diverse workforce.

Important aspects of retention include on-the-job training, opportunity for challenging work, opportunity for advancement, flexible scheduling, competitive compensation, and other monetary and nonmonetary rewards. With an increasingly diverse and changing workforce, supervisors are faced with new challenges. Issues related to single parent households, dual career parents, individuals or families developing relationships, sandwiched employees, older workers, gay and lesbian employees, and individuals with outside commitments are increasingly common dilemmas for human resources offices, for employees, and for supervisors.[14] Many libraries have made a commitment to providing staff with ongoing opportunities to develop the skills they need to function effectively in a diverse workplace. Check to see about training opportunities at your library or larger organization.

## Conclusion

Today diversity is about much more than just affirmative action programs. Affirmative action, while providing a framework to ensure fairness in hiring, has limited influence regarding long-term organizational change. Successful supervisors in diverse organizations possess attributes and skills that are not necessarily of great importance in more traditional organizations. These attributes and skills, sometimes described as core competencies or key behaviors, will enable supervisors to effectively manage staff and to move units and departments forward. Continuing to operate as usual, without taking advantage of the opportunities that a diverse workforce offers, will result in a unit falling behind institutional initiatives.

As a supervisor, you must be prepared to work with a varied and diverse staff. You should be aware of your own opinions or biases and how they might influence your interactions with staff who hold different values.

Flexibility and creativity will be key in this regard. When you treat people as individuals with their own strengths and you value each person's strengths, you will be well on your way to creating a climate that encourages and respects diversity. Figure 6-1 gives some helpful advice on what to do and what to avoid when supervising a diverse workforce.[15]

**FIGURE 6-1  ■  Diversity Do's, Don'ts, and Other Advice**

### DO'S

Be sensitive to differences among people.

Treat everyone with interest, compassion, and sincere concern.

Encourage everyone to participate (and be supportive, especially if they are shy).

Solve tough problems privately.

Hold all staff accountable for minority and equity issues.

Admit we are all prejudiced about something and learn to overcome your own.

Be willing to say, "If I show prejudices, let me know."

Take all people seriously.

If you are having a problem, don't ignore it, seek assistance. Ask colleagues, the equity office or equivalent, for help.

Become a multiculturally sensitive supervisor and encourage others to also be advocates.

### DON'TS

Don't use these differences to form or respond to stereotypes.

Don't jump to conclusions based on stereotypes.

Don't (or allow others to) stereotype or make jokes about people of color.

Don't (or allow others to) stereotype or make jokes about women.

Don't treat minority staff differently.

Don't express amazement when minority staff or women do well.

Don't be confrontational in public.

Don't expect all African Americans or any ethnic group to have a particular accent or the same accent.

Don't use minority or female examples just as extremes (i.e., always negatively).

Don't single out minority staff to answer minority questions; the same goes for women.

Don't use power to hide personal mistakes.

---

## OTHER ADVICE

Differences do exist among people.

These differences do affect how individuals interact in the workplace.

Be observant of interpersonal interactions.

Cultivate the habit of noticing details of these interactions.

Be especially observant about how you interact with your unit or department.

Watch details such as eye contact and your pattern of involving staff.

Create a context where people have names and distinct identities.

Talk privately to staff who are always silent.

Be careful about giving differential attention.

Be extremely careful about casual remarks (especially those made quickly or stressfully).

Learn to recognize your own racist and sexist language.

Avoid racist and sexist language, correct others who use it, and ask that you yourself be corrected.

Seek out minority colleagues in your field for assistance.

---

## NOTES

The epigraph is from Marcus Buckingham and Donald O. Clifton, *Now, Discover Your Strengths* (New York: Free Press, 2001), xx.

**1.** Janice R. W. Joplin and Catherine S. Daus, "Challenges of Leading a Diverse Workforce," *Academy of Management Executive* 11, no. 3 (1997): 32–47.

**2.** Bob Rosner, *The Boss's Survival Guide* (New York: McGraw-Hill, 2001), 187.

**3.** Martha E. Bernal, ed., *Valuing Diversity in Faculty: A Guide* (Washington, D.C.: American Psychological Association, 1996).

**4.** Taylor Cox, *Creating the Multicultural Organization: A Strategy for Capturing the Power of Diversity* (San Francisco: Jossey-Bass, 2001), 6.

**5.** Virgil Larson, "Age Differences Key to Motivation," *Omaha World Herald*, March 17, 2003.

**6.** Neil Howe and William Strauss, *Millennials Go to College: Strategies for a New Generation on Campus: Recruiting and Admissions, Campus Life, and the Classroom* (Washington, D.C.: American Association of Collegiate Registrars and Admissions Officers, and LifeCourse Associates, 2003).

7. Deborah Tannen, *You Just Don't Understand: Women and Men in Conversation* (New York: Ballantine Books, 1990), 43–44.

8. Sally Helgesen, *The Female Advantage: Women's Ways of Leadership* (New York: Doubleday Books, 1990), 19–24.

9. Gordon Lawrence, *People Types and Tiger Stripes* (Gainesville, Fla.: Center for Applications of Psychological Type, 1996).

10. Buckingham and Clifton, *Now, Discover Your Strengths,* 8.

11. Ibid., 81.

12. Ibid., 171.

13. Ibid., 174.

14. Ellen Ernst Kossek and Sharon A. Lobel, eds., *Managing Diversity: Human Resource Strategies for Transforming the Workplace* (Cambridge, Mass.: Blackwell, 1996), 230.

15. The figure is adapted from "Thoughts on Diversity by UNL Faculty," a University of Nebraska-Lincoln internal document for campus faculty.

# 7

# Policies and the Legal Environment

**P**olicies and procedures are an organization's way of defining roles and responsibilities. They set the boundaries for individual actions, defining how managers interact with the organization. Many of these policies are developed to address legal issues and to outline how the organization implements various laws and regulations.

As a manager you need to be aware of the legal responsibilities you have and to know how your organization handles those legal issues. You will also want to know what assistance you can expect from the organization if you do have a problem, and what liabilities you face as a manager. While you may be tempted to hide from legal issues, and try to avoid conflicts that can result from different interpretations of policies and rules, as a manager, you are legally responsible for responding to problem situations. Not acting on personnel issues, for example, can be as dangerous for you individually as is taking the wrong action. For example, if you are aware of a case of alleged sexual harassment in your organization, even if it is not in your unit, and you do not report it, you could still be liable. Once you as a manager are aware of a problem, the organization is assumed to be aware of the problem. Failure to act can result in the employee winning a complaint or suit against the organization because you neglected to act.

Rather than running away from your role as manager in order to avoid legal entanglements, you can significantly decrease the chances of things going awry by following good personnel management practices. You can protect yourself as a supervisor when you create a collaborative working environment instead of a litigious environment.

## United States Employment Laws

Employment laws are numerous and complex, since there is a variety of federal laws, state laws, executive orders, and local laws and regulations regarding the selection of employees and the treatment of individuals in the workplace.[1] Some of these laws apply only when an organization reaches a certain number of employees, while other laws apply to all organizations. The laws and regulations in the employment area change as new laws are passed, as courts render decisions, and as regulations are rewritten. It is your responsibility to remain current on changes in employment laws. Work with your organization's personnel and legal departments to stay abreast of changes that impact your organization. If your organization does not have the support systems you need, seek assistance from county or state offices, local, state, and national library associations, and other business and professional associations that can help you. Not knowing the law is not a valid excuse for acting inappropriately or not acting at all.

Many employment laws and regulations seek to protect employees from discrimination and harassment. Numerous laws and regulations exist that define this important policy area and define fairness in the workplace. Many of the policies that organizations have relating to fairness started with the Civil Rights Act of 1964, which included the concept of equal employment opportunities (EEO). The many guidelines surrounding EEO policies are meant to provide for equal opportunities for all without regard to race, religion, origin, or gender. Many organizations have also added sexual orientation to the list. EEO guidelines apply to hiring decisions, pay, promotion decisions, and firing decisions, as well as to how you manage the work within your unit. As a manager you want to be sure that you are not discriminating against an individual because of that person's characteristics.

Another important law that you need to understand is the Fair Labor Standards Act passed in 1938, which outlines compensation issues, defines the forty-hour workweek, sets a minimum wage, overtime pay, and defines exempt and nonexempt employees. Exempt employees are not covered by the requirements of the act. Exempt employees may meet the following guidelines. They

- are salaried employees
- have hiring and firing authority
- direct the work of others
- make their own decisions about how to do job tasks
- spend most of their time engaged in management duties

Nonexempt employees are covered by the regulations of the Fair Labor Standards Act.

As a supervisor, be sure you are not asking nonexempt employees to work overtime unless they are compensated to do so. You will also want to be sure that employees correctly record their time worked so that overtime is properly identified. It is not useful to have employees, for whatever reason, decide that they will simply work extra hours and not record the time. The organization is still responsible for ensuring that staff are appropriately paid. As a supervisor, you need to be sure that staff follow the rules so that the organization is not liable for violating the law.

The Equal Pay Act of 1963 also addresses the question of compensation and clarifies the concept of equal pay for equal work. This law prohibits an organization from paying women less than men for the same position and job tasks.

The Age Discrimination in Employment Act of 1967 makes it illegal for an organization to discriminate against people who are forty or over. As the workforce in libraries ages, and as staff postpone retirement, accusations of discrimination based on age could increase. Be sure you are not inadvertently discounting the contributions of older employees, stereotyping your staff, or withholding advancement opportunities for staff as they age.

The Americans with Disabilities Act passed in 1990 protects staff with disabilities from discrimination. The definition of "disability" is fairly broad and covers a wide range of conditions. The act also established the concept of "reasonable accommodations" for individuals with disabilities. Employers are required to make reasonable accommodations for a "disabled" person who is qualified for the position, unless doing so causes undue hardship to the employer's business. The person does have to be able to perform the essential functions of the position. Therefore, it is very important that the job description for the position incorporates all of the essential functions of that position. Be sure to keep up with changes in this area as case law develops and the boundaries of the act are clarified.

Another law important to understand is the Family and Medical Leave Act. Passed in 1993, it provides for job-protected leave for family or medical reasons as defined in the act. The reasons for using family and medical leave (FML) may include a serious health condition that makes an employee unable to perform their job duties; the need to care for a spouse, child, or parent who has a serious health condition; and the need to care for an employee's child after birth, adoption, or foster care. Check with your organization to find out when FML may be used and how the organization outlines the reasons for using this type of leave. At a minimum, a person's position is protected for up to twelve weeks of family and medical leave per rolling calendar year. The leave may be with or without pay, depending on the organization's leave policies. Organizations need to have policies on how they implement FML, and you will want to be sure you understand how the law is handled in your organization.

These laws address some of the common issues you face as a supervisor. They do not cover all of the legal issues you need to know as a manager, however. To find out more about which laws affect your work, consult with the human resources experts in your organization. Know when you should contact legal counsel for advice. Perhaps the best course of action as a manager is to remember that if you have any doubts about how to handle a personnel issue, ask for help rather than guess. Making a mistake or avoiding a legal issue can be disastrous to you and the organization. Asking for help and getting legal advice can save you time and decrease the chances that problems will escalate.

## Avoiding Legal Quagmires

One way to avoid legal quagmires is to create a positive working environment for your staff and to practice good personnel management. When employees know the organization's policies regarding the many aspects of employment law, and your staff know that you are consistently following those policies, you are less likely to have problems. Employees become concerned when they feel they are not being treated fairly. The challenge for you as a supervisor is to figure out what defines fair treatment within your unit and in your organization.

### What Is Fair?

Definitions of the word "fair" include terms such as "reasonable," "unbiased," "done properly," and "free from self-interest or prejudice." Notice that being fair is not treating everyone the same. Nor is it treating everyone equally. Rather, fairness means treating people as individuals while following standards and policies. Fairness means that everyone has the opportunity to compete for positions, rewards, and advancement. It does not mean that everyone will advance. Staff will have the opportunity to apply for or seek new challenges, but this does not mean that everyone will succeed.

To create a unit where staff feel they are treated fairly, the rules and guidelines for how decisions are made, how staff are evaluated, and how promotions are granted need to be clear and understandable. When staff understand the rules, they are more likely to understand how decisions are made and why they may or may not get a promotion or other rewards.

When guidelines are clear, it is easier to show that personnel decisions are made as objectively as possible. For example, if you are responsible for recommending merit salary increases, then staff should understand what factors are taken into account when making these decisions. If the performance evaluation is the basis for increases, then it will be important to demonstrate how the evaluation scores translate into dollar or percentage increases in salaries. If you cannot explain how you made your recommendations on merit increases, then you will be creating an environment that will foster suspicion. You will not be seen as fair by your staff.

## *Discrimination*

A perceived lack of fairness can result in accusations of discrimination or harassment. Discrimination and harassment are complex areas that you need to understand as a manager. You need to know your own biases and be sure you are not making decisions or taking actions based on them. While you may not be able to eliminate your own biases, you can understand them and can refrain from using a prejudiced view in the workplace.

Besides understanding your own biases, as a manager you need to understand the complex legal perspective of discrimination and harassment. Again, know your organization's policies in this area. Be sure you are clear on how to recognize and respond to inappropriate behavior in the workplace. Failure to act on cases of discrimination or harassment could make you as liable as the person who is exhibiting the inappropriate behavior.[2]

To help create an environment where it is clear that discrimination and harassment will not be tolerated, you can use the following practices.

Act when you hear about behavior that makes you suspicious. Talk to employees who may be involved in inappropriate actions, or find out what has occurred. Remind staff about the organization's policies on workplace behavior. Take appropriate actions based on organizational policy and procedures.

Encourage staff to report incidences of inappropriate behavior. Help staff understand that reporting problems is not "tattling" on fellow workers, but is protecting all members of the unit and organization from potential problems.

Investigate or report complaints that come to you, following organizational policies and procedures. Do not dismiss a complaint because you cannot imagine the staff member behaving inappropriately.

Do not tolerate inappropriate jokes and stories. Nothing in the workplace is "just kidding."[3]

Most important, document your actions. You will need the written evidence if you pursue an investigation, and if the organization is to take action and then show that appropriate action was taken.

Handling accusations of discrimination or harassment can be touchy. You can be successful when you carefully follow your organization's policies, when you consult with the proper authorities, when you document what you have done, and when you take time to carefully address the problem. These problems will not go away. You must address them in order to resolve them and to create or re-create a positive working environment.

## Handling Complaints

Despite your best efforts to demonstrate fairness, staff members may still feel that they are not receiving the same benefits as others in the unit. Complaints may arise when someone in the unit receives a promotion, a larger raise, or additional training opportunities. When you are faced with a staff member questioning your actions, you can handle the situation most effectively by taking time to listen carefully to the staff member and being prepared to explain your decision. The steps you take will depend on how your organization handles any particular problem. However, in any situation, you need to actively address the issue. This is not the time to hide or try to cover up a problem. The sooner the organization can address a problem, the more likely the issue will be successfully resolved.

What are some ways you can begin to address this type of concern? Imagine you are deciding whom to promote in your unit. You have two possible internal candidates, Sally and Jane. Based on their qualifications, you choose Sally. However, Jane believes she should have gotten the promotion, since she has been in the unit longer. Jane accuses you of being unfair. What should you do? When faced with an accusation of unfairness regarding a promotion decision, try the following techniques.

Plan ahead for potential questions by having a clear set of criteria for personnel decisions. Be sure that job postings and ads for promotion opportunities outline the skills needed for the position and the qualifications that are sought.

Prepare for a conversation with an unhappy staff member by reviewing your notes about how you made your decision. This is not the time to guess at what you did or to be vague about the process you used to make a decision.

Focus on the staff member who has questioned the decision, and not on the person who received the promotion. Maintain confidential information and do not reveal personal information about the successful candidate. In other words, do not explain why the other person got the promotion.

Instead, explain what skills were needed and review the qualifications as noted in the announcement of the position. Then review the staff member's performance regarding those skills. This approach assumes you have documented any skills or performance issues in the annual performance review. This way you can refer to written documentation that the person has already seen to illustrate your points about skills.

Be direct and factual, yet sensitive to the person's feelings. Treat the staff member with respect. Focus on the person's strengths and how he or she can improve their performance and develop the skills needed for other promotional opportunities. However, be very careful not to promise the person that he or she will succeed the next time they apply for a promotion.

Discuss development plans and career goals with the staff member. Turn the conversation into an opportunity to help the person with career planning.

Do not expect the staff member to agree with your decision or to thank you for the conversation. Instead, give the person time to reflect on the conversation.

Follow up later with the staff member about ideas for career development. Help the staff member find ways to use his or her strengths to excel and therefore possibly qualify for rewards and advancement opportunities.

Fairness is all about helping staff to become the best employees they can become. If you are consistent in how you apply policies and rules, and are clear about your expectations for workplace behavior, you will go a long way toward creating an environment that helps staff feel they are respected and are being treated fairly.

### Why Problems Develop

Problems can develop in an organization when the top management and the organization do not take time to generate and implement appropriate personnel policies and procedures. But procedures alone will not resolve problems. Once policies and procedures are in place, management must ensure that the following occur:[4]

*Appropriate training.* Inadequate training of supervisors increases the chances that they will not respond appropriately to problems.

*Following written agreements.* Not adhering to written contracts and union agreements will result in problems for the manager and the organization.

*Consistent enforcement of procedures.* Policies and procedures apply to all members of the unit. Excusing poor performance by one person while expecting compliance by others will result in problems.

*Clear understanding of fair treatment.* Perceived unfairness will cause staff unrest and create problems for the unit and the manager.

As a supervisor, take time to learn about employment laws, policies, and regulations. Then follow the policies in a consistent manner. You will be more successful as a supervisor when you are perceived to be fair.


## Conclusion

As a manager, you are responsible for knowing and following your organization's policies, particularly those that are based on employment laws. Employment laws change as current cases are decided, regulations are written, or legislative action occurs. Be sure you keep informed about changes that affect your workplace. Ignorance of the law is not an excuse for inappropriate actions. When in doubt, seek advice from your personnel office or legal counsel.

Your best defense as a supervisor is to be fair and to be consistent. Creating a good working environment where staff are productive and feel respected will go a long way toward eliminating potential legal problems.

### NOTES

**1.** Gary McClain and Deborah S. Romaine, *The Everything Managing People Book* (Avon, Mass.: Adams Media, 2000), 204.

**2.** Ibid., 211.

**3.** Ibid., 212.

**4.** Daryl Leaming, *Academic Leadership* (Boston: Anker, 1998), 111–12.

# 8

# Hiring and Interviewing

Jane has just been given the task of heading a new three-person team in the library to develop a program to help patrons search, create, and use image databases. Jane gets to hire two new librarians to work on her team. She would like to call up a few friends from library school to work with her on this project, but she cannot do that. Jane's organization requires that she do a national or regional search to find the best people for the job. Jane has never conducted a search before. What should she do? Jane asks the human resources staff for help.

Determining the work that needs to be accomplished and selecting employees to do that work are two of the most important responsibilities of a supervisor. Whether you are filling an existing vacancy or are fortunate to have an entirely new position, consider carefully what sort of work you would like the incumbent to accomplish. Your library or larger organization very likely has guidelines for writing a job description, advertising a position, interviewing applicants, and making a hiring decision. Working within these guidelines, you will be able to interview and hire the best candidate for your position opening.

## Job Descriptions

The hiring process begins with a good job description. Job descriptions include the basic functions of the position and serve a variety of purposes. For supervisors, the job description provides a framework for staff performance evaluations. For the employee, the job description identifies the essential job functions and helps the employee to understand what is expected of them.

Job descriptions should include a job summary, a detailed list of duties and responsibilities, necessary qualifications, and, if pertinent, any physical requirements for the position. The listing of duties and responsibilities should be detailed enough that a new employee can understand the tasks to be accomplished. Many job descriptions include the percentage of time devoted to each task, as well as an indication of whether the task is essential to the position. The use of clear, concise, and consistent language is very important for delineating duties and responsibilities, particularly when the same task may be done by more than one employee.[1]

For Jane, developing job descriptions for her new positions is a challenge. Still, she needs to outline the key tasks of the job and the qualifications that are needed. For these digital reference positions, Jane might ask for previous experience with image databases or software packages, with creating websites, or experience on digitization projects. Because these are entry-level positions, Jane may list prior experience under "preferred qualifications" and seek people with a strong interest in technology instead of experience.

## Hiring Processes

Libraries, like all employers, have requirements and guidelines for hiring that are related to federal employment and equal opportunity legislation. If you work in a large library, there may be a human resources person or department in the organization. For some public libraries, the city government's human resources office may be the source for guidelines and regulations. For small college or university libraries, the central campus's human resources office may handle personnel for the entire campus. Depending on the situation in your library, work with the appropriate human resources personnel or department to be sure that you are following all the necessary procedures.

## *Preparing for the Interview*

Prior to interviewing a candidate, review the requirements of the job. Review the position description (which lists the specific tasks to be performed on the job, as well as the methods, techniques, technology, and tools or equipment used to accomplish these tasks). Make note of unusual working conditions and other specific demands of the job, in order to adapt the interview to elicit relevant information.

Develop your interview questions well in advance and relate those questions to the requirements of the job. Even experienced supervisors may occasionally wonder about the appropriateness of asking particular questions. The best advice to follow is that if a question is not job-related, do not ask it. Questions about an applicant's name; address; age; race, color, or national origin; gender; religion or creed; sexual orientation; citizenship; marital, parental, or family status; military service; criminal record; and disability should not be asked unless they pertain to the job. For example, if you need to verify degree or past employment information, it is all right to ask whether an applicant's work records are under another name, for the purpose of access to those records. However, you should not ask the ethnic origin of a name, if a woman is a Miss, Mrs., or Ms., or request a maiden name. Because diversity is such an important issue in today's libraries, and we want to convey this to our job applicants, it may be tempting to ask questions related to a candidate's ethnicity at interviews. It is permissible to state that your library is an equal opportunity employer. However, you should not ask anything that would require a candidate to indicate race, color, national origin, or gender. For additional examples of legal and illegal questions, see the quiz in figure 8-1.

FIGURE 8-1 ■ Legal and Illegal Questions: A Quiz

**Question**
You are interviewing a woman for a position in your circulation department. She mentioned during the interview that she is a single parent. Because the position requires a weekend shift once each month, is it okay to ask, "Can you arrange for child care?"

**Answer**
NO. Even though she volunteered the information about having children, this question is not appropriate. However, you can ask if she is willing to work the required schedule.

**Question**

You are interviewing a man for a position in your access services department. Because he will be responsible for collecting money from photocopy machines, is it permissible to ask him, "Have you ever been arrested?"

**Answer**

NO. However, it is okay to ask him if he has ever been convicted of theft, because the crime is related to the position. Convictions, if related to the position, are pertinent. Arrests, however, are not.

**Question**

You want to hire a cataloger for foreign language materials and need to know what languages the applicant can read and at what level. Is it permissible to ask a question such as, "What languages do you read fluently?"

**Answer**

YES. This question is perfectly acceptable because the answer is relevant to the performance of the job.

Carefully review the application and resume prior to the interview. Familiarity with the candidate's application paperwork, so that you don't have to refer to it often during the interview, will allow you to concentrate on asking questions and listening carefully to the candidate's answers.

## Conducting the Interview

The climate created in the interview is important. Create a welcoming atmosphere, away from noise and interruptions. Introduce yourself to the candidate. Determine the candidate's preferred name and use it during the interview. Set a tone for a friendly exchange of comments and allow communication to develop freely in order to build mutual confidence.[2]

Describe the job and the library. Keep in mind that an interview is a two-way process. The candidate needs to know about the position, your department, salary information, training opportunities, and other information that will help him or her to make a decision about accepting the position if it is offered. You want to learn as much as possible about the candidate's qualifications for the position.

Asking applicants for examples from their past work history or educational experiences will reveal areas of knowledge, skills, and abilities that are required for them to perform the job successfully. By the close of the interview you want to have an accurate and balanced picture of the applicant's qualifications and job motivation. Behavioral, situational, and competency-based interview questions will provide the best information for determining if the applicant can do the job. If you have a formal set of core competencies for your library or unit, it is important to ask questions that will be helpful in determining whether your applicant meets or could meet a level of competency in areas important to your unit. Regardless of whether you have formal competencies, you will most likely have a set of knowledge, skills, behaviors, and attributes (the components of formal core competencies lists) that are important for the particular position and important to your organization. To elicit information about candidates' knowledge, skills, behaviors, and attributes, you might ask the following questions.[3]

If analytical skills or problem-solving is a competency, examples of questions to consider asking include:

> Walk me through a situation in which you had to get information by asking many questions of several people. How did you know what to ask?
>
> Describe a time you had to ask questions and listen carefully to clarify the exact nature of an internal or external customer's problem.

If creativity is a competency, you might ask:

> Tell me about a way in which you worked with other staff to develop creative ideas to solve problems.
>
> Describe how you've gone about learning a new technical task.
>
> In your current position, what have you done differently than your predecessors?
>
> Tell me about a creative idea you had to improve a library service.
>
> Tell me about a unique approach you took to solve a problem.

If working in groups (teamwork) is important for the position, consider asking:

> Can you give me an example of a group decision you were involved in recently? What did you do to help the group reach the decision?
>
> Describe a time you worked with a group or team to determine project responsibilities. What was your role?

If you value flexibility and adaptability in employees in your unit, consider asking:

> Tell me about an important project, task, or assignment you were working on in which the specifications changed. (What did you do? How did it affect you?)
>
> Tell me about a time you had to meet a scheduled deadline while your work was being continually interrupted. What caused you to have the most difficulty and why?
>
> Going from [position] to [position] must have been difficult. Tell me about a challenge that occurred when making that transition. (How did you handle it?)
>
> Describe a time you had to significantly modify work procedures to align with new strategic directives.

To determine leadership ability or potential, consider asking:

> Tell me about a time you inspired someone to work hard to do a good job.
>
> Describe a face-to-face meeting in which you had to lead or influence a very sensitive individual.
>
> Tell me about a time you were able to convince someone from outside (your department, etc.) to cooperate with you on an important project.
>
> What strategies have you used to communicate a major change to employees? Which strategies have worked and which have not?
>
> Describe a situation in which you had to translate a broad or general plan into specific goals.

For positions where customer service is important, consider asking:

> In your current job, how do you know if your internal or external customers are satisfied? (Give a specific example.)
>
> Tell me about a time when you were able to respond to an internal or external customer's request in a shorter period of time than expected. Contrast that situation with a time when you failed to meet a customer's expectations. (What was the difference?)
>
> As a [position], how did you ensure that you were providing good service?

Sometimes it's necessary to work with a customer who has unusual requests. Please describe a time when you had to handle an unusual request that seemed unreasonable. What did you do?

Some days can be very busy with requests from customers and co-workers. Please describe an occasion recently when you didn't have enough time to completely satisfy a particular customer. How did you handle the situation?

If planning skills are critical to the position, consider asking:

Walk me through yesterday (or last week) and tell me how you planned the day's (or week's) activities.

What procedure have you used to keep track of items that need attention? Tell me about a time you used that procedure.

What objectives did you set for this year? (What steps have you taken to make sure that you're making progress on all of them?)

Sometimes deadlines don't allow the luxury of carefully considering all options before making a decision. Please give an example of a time this happened to you. What was the result of your decision?

Tell me about a time you were faced with conflicting priorities. In scheduling your time, how did you determine what was a priority?

To determine the applicant's level of technical knowledge or expertise, consider asking:

Describe a project, situation, or assignment that challenged your skills as a [position]. What did you do to effectively manage the situation?

Sometimes complex projects require additional expertise. Describe a situation in which you had to request help.

Have you ever had to orient a new employee on a technical task or area? How did you do it?

Describe a time you solved a technical problem.

What equipment have you been trained to operate? How proficient are you?

What word-processing packages can you use? How proficient are you?

Give me an example of a project that demonstrates your technical expertise in [web page development].

Describe how you've gone about learning a new technical task.

How much experience have you had operating a [mouse, keyboard, word processor, etc.]?

Describe the most challenging work you've done.

To determine the level of a candidate's interpersonal skills, considering asking:

Working with people from diverse backgrounds or cultures can present specific challenges. Can you tell me about a time you faced a challenge adapting to a person from a different background or culture? (What happened? What did you do? What was the result?)

Our relationships with coworkers are not always perfect. Tell me about the most challenging relationship you had with a coworker. Why was it challenging? What did you do to try to make it work?

In addition to the kinds of questions just outlined, Jane will want to ask specific questions about her candidates' technology interests and skills. Jane may find that a candidate who is enthusiastic and willing to learn may be a better fit for this new venture than someone with impressive technical skills but poor interpersonal skills. In other words, hire talent and remember that you can teach skills. Recruiting an enthusiastic learner can be more successful in the long run than someone who does not fit well in the organization and is not enthusiastic about the challenge of starting a new project.

During the interview, your job is to listen, ask follow-up questions when necessary, and evaluate the candidate's answers to try to predict future performance. Practice good communication skills such as active listening, reflecting, and reframing, and you will learn much about the candidate.

If you find the candidate is giving short answers and you are not learning enough about the person, ask follow-up questions. Continue to probe the answers until you feel comfortable that you have learned all you need to from the candidate. Candidates can be quite nervous, particularly if they are new to the job market. You can help the person by asking questions that help them explain their skills and interests. Do not settle for a "yes" or "no" answer if you want more information. Ask again if needed. This is your chance to learn about the candidate. Don't be shy. Ask and ask and ask and listen and listen and listen.

When you have finished asking your list of questions, ask the candidate if they have any additional information related to the position that they would like you to know. This gives the applicant the chance to mention or reiterate any strengths they bring to the position. Then ask the candidate if he or she has any questions for you.

If an applicant voluntarily offers information that you would never ask for legal reasons (see the quiz questions in figure 8-1), human resources specialists recommend that you not write down the information they volunteer. Instead, guide the interview back to issues specifically related to the job.

At the end of the interview, thank the applicant for their interest in the position, outline what will happen next, and give the applicant a sense of when you will make your decision.

### After the Interview

After the interview, note your impressions of the job candidate and his or her answers to the questions you posed. Complete this task as soon as possible after the interview, particularly when you are interviewing more than one applicant.

Once you have completed all the interviews and are assessing the results to decide which candidate best fits the requirements for the position, remember to check applicants' references if you have not already done so. Many organizations require that supervisors check references prior to making an employment offer. Even if this is not a requirement at your library, never offer a position to a candidate without checking his or her references first.

### Reference Checks

Conducting reference checks will give you added insight on an applicant's personal characteristics and past job performance (i.e., reliability, attendance, quality of work) and allow you to verify the information that the candidate provided. Make sure you obtain the applicant's consent before calling a former or current employer. If possible, work with your library or larger organization's human resources department to revise application forms to require applicants to list all previous employers, dates of employment, positions held, names of supervisors, and reasons for departure. It is important to be consistent in conducting all reference checks.

When checking references, keep notes about the names contacted, what questions were asked, and what answers you received. And, as with interview questions for applicants, the same questions should be asked for each applicant's references. Developing a standardized form, or script, can make reference checks very systematic and easy to conduct. Use the reference check to verify factual information, such as dates of employment.

The following is a sample script for a reference check.

---

Hello. My name is [your name] and I work at [Such-and-Such Library]. We are interviewing for a [position] and would like to verify employment information on [applicant's name], who was employed by you from [beginning date] until [ending date].

What was the nature of his or her job?

What did you think of his or her work?

What are his or her strong points?

What are his or her weak points?

How did he or she get along with other people?

Would you comment on his or her: attendance; dependability; ability to take on responsibility; ability to follow instructions; degree of supervision needed; overall attitude; quality of work; quantity of work?

Why did he or she leave the position?

Would you reemploy him or her? If no, why not?

Is there anything else you would like to comment on regarding [applicant's name] employment or job performance?

---

## Conclusion

Hiring decisions are some of the most important decisions you will make as a manager or supervisor. You will be most successful when you

- carefully think through the requirements of the position
- clearly state the job requirements in the ad
- ask behavioral questions that are job-related
- listen carefully to interviewees
- hire talent and train for skills
- know your own biases and guard against making decisions based on them

■ ask legal questions and avoid non-work-related questions

When you hire the right people for the right jobs, you will have the solid foundation you need for a successful unit or department.

## NOTES

1. Beth McNeil, "Managing Work Performance and Career Development: Implications for Human Resources in Academic Libraries," in *Human Resource Management in Today's Academic Library: Meeting Challenges and Creating Opportunities,* ed. Janice Simmons-Welburn and Beth McNeil (Westport, Conn.: Libraries Unlimited, 2004).

2. Thyra Russell, "Interviewing," in *Practical Help for New Supervisors,* ed. Joan Giesecke (Chicago: American Library Association, 1997).

3. University Libraries, University of Nebraska-Lincoln, internal document on core competency-related interview questions.

# 9
# Orientation and Training

**N**ow that the search is over and you have filled the job opening in your unit, you may think your work is done. Not quite! You must orient the new employee to your library. An effective orientation will include introductions to current staff and an introduction to policies and procedures. It will also provide an opportunity for the new person to begin to get to know the culture of the organization. The new employee's orientation, in particular the first day on the job, can influence how that person will feel about the library throughout his or her employment.[1]

The details of an orientation program will vary depending on the type and size of your library, as well as the nature of the position. However, many libraries share common goals for new employee orientation, as summarized by H. Scott Davis in his book *New Employee Orientation,* including:

> To make all new library employees feel welcome and comfortable as they begin the new job;

> To provide consistent documentation and interpretation of major library policies and philosophies for all new employees and, in the course of doing so, strive to avoid "information overload";

To acquaint all new library employees with other library staff and other departments and units within the library system;

To provide continuing orientation support to all new employees during the initial months of their employment through mentoring and other activities;

To tailor individual orientation activities/information according to the varying information needs for different positions within the library and, in doing so, to be mindful of individual differences among new employees in terms of personal experience and educational background;

To emphasize the new employee's role and potential for contributing to the overall mission of the unit/department, division, and library, and, finally;

To call attention to the importance of continuing staff development and the library's commitment to staff training, and to emphasize new employees' share of responsibility in self-initiating/communicating staff development needs to their supervisor.[2]

## Orientation

Preparations for an orientation of a new employee should start as soon as you have made a hiring decision, if not before. Planning includes both in-house preparation and communication with your new employee. Your library may have a general orientation for all new employees. Check with your supervisor or the library human resources specialist to find out about the standard orientation procedures in your library.

Before the employee's first day, you will want to review the job description and the job duties or responsibilities for that position, and make any necessary changes to them. These two documents are crucial to the success of the new employee, so that they will know what is expected of them and how their work fits into the larger organization. Carefully plan how you will explain the job and its duties to the new employee.

You may want to consider generational differences when planning the orientation of a new employee. The youngest group of library workers today, born in the 1980s or later, often referred to as generation Y or millennials, is used to learning in a highly interactive way. Like their slightly older coworkers from the generation X group, they may like to role-play, finding it to be good practice for real-life skills. For example, if you are training generation Y or generation X staff to work at a public service desk, role-playing situations with difficult patrons might prove to be a very effective training tool. When orienting employees born in the mid-1960s through 1979 or so (i.e., generation X), a less structured training plan for orientation may be helpful. If you plan to walk them through your library's policy and procedure documents, you might consider instead showing them the files (binders, library staff website, etc.) and encouraging them to review them. Keep in mind that the average generation X staff member is not afraid to ask questions. Consider providing a list of in-house experts so that when the new employee has a question, he or she can go directly to the right source for the answer.

For new employees from the baby boomer and veteran generations, discuss your library's overall goals. Boomers will want to know how they fit into those goals. Baby boomers like to see themselves as making a difference, and as an important part of a larger, worthwhile effort. When you are discussing the upcoming challenges, convey that you will need their help. Individuals in this age group want to solve problems. Veterans also want to contribute. With them, you may want to convey not only the unit and organization goals, but also tell them the history of the department and the library: where the library is coming from and where it is trying to go. Veterans, more so than baby boomers and much more so than generation X employees, want to know the policies and guidelines of your unit and library. They will desire a very detailed orientation and training program and will want a more structured orientation than younger generations.[3]

If your library has in place a set list of orientation meetings for new employees, you will want to supplement it with sessions pertinent to the new employee's particular job. Depending on the nature of the position, and your library's policies, the orientation period may last anywhere from a few weeks to several months. Some meetings can take place during the first week, and others in subsequent weeks. Some details should be handled on the first day at work. Prior to the new employee's first day on the job, you will want to schedule as many meetings as possible for him or her to meet with colleagues in the unit and in the library.

### Sample Schedule for First Day

The following is a sample schedule for a new employee.

> Sophie Fishfeather
> Library Assistant, Acquisitions Unit
> Townsville Public Library

*Day 1*—Thursday, March 1

8:00 a.m.   Meet Jean Smith at library's entry

Introduction to unit. Review of orientation schedule. Review of personnel policies, department procedures, and other general information

10:30 a.m.   Tour of library with Fiona Birdcup
                (acquisitions assistant)

12 noon   Lunch with Jean Smith

1:00 p.m.   Unit staff meeting

2:00 p.m.   Library Human Resources Department
              (for employment paperwork)

2:45 p.m.   Library director

3:00 p.m.   Walter Bauxbiter (mailroom manager)

3:30 p.m.   Pete Hare (serials check-in)

4:00 p.m.   Review of first day

5:00 p.m.   End of day one!

## Orientation Checklists

As a supervisor, you may find it helpful to use an orientation checklist for new employees. Your library may have a general checklist that you can tailor to your unit's needs; if not, develop one for your unit. The checklist might include people to meet within the unit, the library, and outside the library; meetings to attend; and projects or programs with which to become familiar as soon as possible. The checklist may also include the names of those responsible for particular aspects of orientation and whether or not that item or function is required or optional.

Orientation checklists can be used as a supervisory planning tool prior to the employee's first day of work. They can also serve as the written orientation plan that you give to the new employee during your first meeting with them. Some, like the one shown in figure 9-1, note when the meetings or activities should take place. Others are less detailed and serve more as a reminder list of meetings that need to be scheduled, such as the sample list for a new reference librarian shown in figure 9-2.

**FIGURE 9-1** ■ **Orientation Checklist**

## TECHNICAL SERVICES DEPARTMENT ORIENTATION CHECKLIST

New Employee:   Sophie Fishfeather
Position:            Library Assistant
Unit:                 Acquisitions Unit
Start Date:         Thursday, March 1, 20___

| Function/Activity | Person Responsible | 1st Day | 1st Week | Subsequent Weeks |
|---|---|---|---|---|
| Review of orientation schedule | Supervisor | X | | |
| Review position description, job duties, and responsibilities | Supervisor | X | | |
| Review personnel policies | Supervisor | X | | |
|    Hours and scheduling | Supervisor | X | | |
|    Time sheets | Supervisor | X | | |
|    Breaks | Supervisor | X | | |
|    Types of leave | Supervisor | X | | |
|    Staff development programs/training | Supervisor | X | | |
|    Use of computers and e-mail | Supervisor | X | | |
|    Other | Supervisor | X | | |
| Tour of library | Department | X | | |
| Introduction to e-mail system and log-on | Systems office | X | | |
| Individual meetings with unit staff | | | | |
|    Fiona Birdcup | Supervisor | | X | |
|    Walter Bauxbiter | Supervisor | X | | |
|    Pete Hare | Supervisor | X | | |
|    T. C. Henry | Supervisor | | X | |
| Individual meetings with staff in other units | | | | |
|    Cataloging supervisor | Supervisor | | | Week 2 |
|    Serials manager | Supervisor | | | Week 2 |
|    Binding manager | Supervisor | | | Week 3 |
|    Etc. | Supervisor | | | Week 3+ |

| Function/Activity | Person Responsible | 1st Day | 1st Week | Subsequent Weeks |
|---|---|---|---|---|
| Orientation to computer network | Systems staff | | X | |
| Employment paperwork | Library admin. | X | | |
| Keys | Library admin. | X | | |
| Parking permit | Library admin. | | X | |
| Online catalog training | Supervisor | | X | |

**FIGURE 9-2** ■ **Orientation Checklist for a New Reference Librarian**

Schedule meeting with 1 department head each week:

_____ Access Services

_____ Technical Services

_____ Systems

_____ Digital Initiatives

Schedule meeting with 1 unit head each week:

_____ Circulation

_____ Interlibrary Loan

_____ Microforms

_____ Documents

_____ Binding

Regularly scheduled meetings to add to calendar:

Reference Dept. meetings (1st and 3rd Thursdays at 1:00 p.m.)

Digital Initiatives Dept. meetings (4th Wednesday at 3:00 p.m.)

Library Faculty meetings (1st Tuesday in September, December, February, and May at 9:00 a.m.)

Other meetings to schedule after librarian is on board:

Organizational units outside the library

## Preparations for Arrival

Prior to the new employee's arrival, prepare their work space. Make certain that the basic equipment and office supplies necessary for the position are in place and ready to use. Basic supplies include desk supplies, such as a stapler and scissors, as well as the necessary ergonomic supplies related to extended computer workstation use. A checklist of supplies for consideration is included in the conclusion at the end of this chapter.

And last, make arrangements with the new employee regarding what time they should report to work on the first day and where you will meet them. Share their orientation schedule with them. If this is not possible, at least provide a schedule for their first day, with confirmation of where and when they should report.

## First Day on the Job

Setting the right tone for the new employee's first day on the job is crucial. At the end of the first day, the new person should feel welcomed to the unit and library, and valued for the skills they bring to the job. They should know the general plan for their orientation and what training to expect in the next few weeks.

A person beginning a new job may be anxious about many things that first day, including everything from how to remember the names of all the people he or she will meet to the scope of the job duties. Your goal is to alleviate that anxiety. When you first meet the new employee, greet them warmly and welcome them to the library. Remind the new employee of your name. Let him or her know how to address you:

"Good morning. I'm Jean Smith. It's good to see you again. We're so glad you're joining us here at the library. As I mentioned during your interview, I'm the manager of the microforms unit and I will be your supervisor. Please call me Jean. May I call you Jane?"

If your name is difficult to pronounce, repeat it and if possible, provide a key to remembering how to pronounce it. Keep this in mind as well when you make introductions to other staff throughout the day.

Review the orientation and training schedule with the new employee. Explain whom they will be meeting with and the purpose of each meeting. Note any regular standing meetings that the new employee should plan to attend.

Introduce the new person to members of the unit and to other staff with whom he or she will work frequently. On the first day, these introductions can be brief. Your orientation schedule will include time for in-depth meetings, i.e., explaining the staff member's work and his or her role in the department, later in the orientation period.

The first day on the job should include a tour of the unit or department and the library. You or another member of the unit can lead the tour. Try to show the employee as much of the library as possible without overwhelming them. During the tour, you may encounter additional staff members to introduce to the new employee. Depending on the size of your library, you may decide to tailor the tour, perhaps saving some parts for future days. At the very minimum you should make sure the employee knows how to find the bathroom, break room, and how to navigate between the unit and the library's entry.

Although you may have shared the position description with the new employee at the time of their interview, you should review it with them again in detail on their first day. Discuss each job duty, the tasks and routines associated with it, and how performance on each duty will be evaluated.

At some point during the first day, you should provide time for the employee to work with your human resources staff to complete the appropriate paperwork to ensure timely payment of salary or wages. Some libraries may handle these details prior to the first day on the job. Check with your human resources specialist to learn the procedures in your library.

And finally, keep in mind that your new employee will need time to familiarize him or herself with their new work space and to review the documentation that you have shared during the day. This "down time" will allow the employee an opportunity to reflect on the meetings and activities of the first day on the job.

## Training

Training is an integral part of orientation. During your initial discussions with the new employee, which include the review of the orientation schedule and the position documents, the new employee should learn more about the specific training necessary for the position. A focus on training during this initial orientation will signify to the employee that you value their ongoing development. Increasingly, the jobs of library staff members are changing to meet the needs of library users. Most positions in today's libraries require ongoing training to stay up-to-date with new software versions, web resources, and other electronic resources. During orientation, it will be important to share with a new staff member your expectations for their attendance at staff development and training events.

As a supervisor, you may be responsible for much of the position-specific training for a new employee. As you consider the content of the training, you may want to decide how to best deliver the training and what to teach the new employee first. Knowing the employee's preferred learning style will help. Questions to consider include the following. "Will the content be understood more easily and retained longer if the employee sees a videotape, completes a workbook, or listens to a presentation? In what sequence should new information be presented? What should we teach the new employee first—how to search a book order or how to process a vendor list? Does it matter?"[4]

Many libraries also provide librarywide training for library staff and librarians. Sometimes this training is organized or developed by the library administration or by a staff development committee or team. The training may be on topics such as customer service, facilitation skills, communication skills building, basic library skills, leadership development, measurement and assessment, team-building, technical skills training, or other efforts related to librarywide goals or library administration initiatives. The library administration may encourage, and sometimes even require, staff participation at training on issues related to organizational culture. Some libraries have developed training or career development plans tailored to individual staff members. Whether you are developing a single training session to address one topic or a multi-session training program for a new employee, effective job-training programs include the following steps:

- analyzing needs
- describing the task
- analyzing the task
- writing objectives
- developing tests
- formulating instructional strategies
- sequencing
- developing materials
- preparing evaluations[5]

By becoming familiar with the staff development planning and opportunities in your library, you will be able to plan for appropriate orientation and ongoing training for the staff you supervise.

## Conclusion

A carefully planned orientation program will help your employees begin their jobs on a positive note and with the information they need to succeed. Remember to include the following in your plans.

*Before the first day*

Communicate with the employee regarding the logistical issues of the first day on the job: when and where to report, work schedule or hours, where to park, etc.

Prepare the work area with supplies:

| | |
|---|---|
| pencils, pens | mouse pad |
| stapler | wrist rest |
| scissors | phone books |
| paper | wastebasket |
| notepads | recycle bin |
| staff directory with phone, e-mail, office address information | computer diskettes |

Assess equipment needs:

| | |
|---|---|
| computer workstation | headphones |
| printer | |

*First day*

Meet and welcome new employee
Introduce employee to coworkers
Provide tour of library
Review job duties and responsibilities

Explain e-mail and phone access

Complete employment paperwork

*First week*

Discuss and review unit or department policies

Provide follow-up tours, depending on size of library

Discuss library goals and objectives, librarywide policies

Provide training in core job areas

*Subsequent weeks*

Meet with pertinent staff members and departments

Ongoing training

## NOTES

**1.** Katherine Branch, "Orienting the New Library Employee," in *Practical Help for New Supervisors,* ed. Joan Giesecke (Chicago: American Library Association, 1997), 15–23.

**2.** H. Scott Davis, *New Employee Orientation: A How-to-Do-It Manual for Librarians* (New York: Neal-Schuman, 1994).

**3.** Ron Zemke, Claire Raines, and Bob Bilipczak, *Generations at Work: Managing the Clash of Veterans, Boomers, Xers, and Nexters in Your Workplace* (New York: AMACOM, 1999).

**4.** Pat L. Weaver-Meyers, "Creating Effective Training Programs," in *Staff Development: A Practical Guide,* 3rd ed., Elizabeth Fuseler Avery, Terry Dahlin, and Deborah A. Carver, eds. (Chicago: American Library Association, 2001), 125.

**5.** Ibid., 125–28.

# 10
# Planning and Organizing Work

**N**ow that you are a supervisor, you are responsible for planning and organizing the work of your unit. Planning can involve everything from day-to-day prioritizing of projects and activities for your staff to decision-making on long-term projects and activities for your unit to meet your larger organization's goals. Planning is an ongoing process that must evolve as the needs of your organization change. You will need to be flexible, and be a model of adaptability and flexibility for the staff you supervise, so that they become accustomed to the rapidly changing environment of today's libraries.

## Setting Goals and Objectives

The goals of your unit or department should relate to the overall goals of your library or larger organization. Many libraries develop librarywide goals as part of an annual planning process. These goals may span several years, with new objectives developed for each year. Departmental goals can follow this pattern. As a supervisor, you will identify the goals of your unit or department, establish priorities among those goals, and identify the tasks that must be accomplished to meet the goals.

Developing objectives for the unit becomes the basis for unit-wide as well as individual planning. Good objectives have the following characteristics, as seen in the acronym SMART: Specific, Measurable, Achievable, Relevant, and Time-bound.[1]

An objective outlines specifically what is to be done (S) and what measures you will use to determine that an objective has been reached (M). The objective should provide the unit with a challenge that is achievable, or can be met (A). You don't want to write objectives that will serve to frustrate your unit because they cannot be completed. Objectives should be relevant, i.e., support the goals of the organization (R), and they should have a time frame attached to them (T). An objective for a circulation unit, for example, would be "to plan and implement a new patron maintenance procedure [S] that is less staff-intensive [M] by the end of the calendar year [T]." Assuming the unit can design its own procedures, the objective is achievable (A) and relevant to the organization (R).

Once you have identified goals and established priorities for your unit, you can determine your own personal goals and work with staff to determine their goals. Goal-setting for your unit, yourself, and your staff is critical to move forward as a unit. You need to decide who will perform which tasks, how often the tasks will need to be performed, and the timetables and deadlines for each task. Staff will need to understand the rewards for accomplishing the tasks and goals, as well as the implications for themselves and the department if tasks are not accomplished and goals not met.

Review and update your unit's action plans regularly, perhaps quarterly, to be sure you are on track for the year. By keeping your focus on overall objectives, you can be sure your unit does not get sidetracked by mundane details and day-to-day tasks and can accomplish the larger projects that bring success to your unit.

For example, Susan heads the access services department in a medium-sized academic library. The library has reviewed and issued its six major goals or initiatives for the year. These are as follow.

1. *Digital scholarship and literacy program.* This program involves creating and sustaining digital collections, organizing and providing access to electronic resources, and providing instruction on how scholarship is changing in the digital age. The instructional component expands the information literacy program to address how information and text function and are understood in digital form.

2. *A user-centered focus for services* continues to place the library user at the center of library planning and service delivery.

3. *The enhancement of collections to support research, instruction, and service* continues the commitment to build and preserve a research-level collection.

4. *Learning organization.* Continue to build a learning organization, where individual learning expands the ability of the library to change and supports improvements in the economies, efficiency, and effectiveness of the organization.

5. *Library as place.* Promote the university library as a place to build community on campus and as the center of scholarship on campus.

6. *Diversify and leverage funding and resources.* Attract additional funding and make the most effective use of library resources, both public and private, to advance the library's mission.

As head of access services, Susan works with her unit to identify objectives and steps they could take in response to each of these goals. (See figure 10-1.)

FIGURE 10-1 ■ Department or Unit Objectives

| Library Goals/Initiatives | Department/Unit Objectives |
|---|---|
| 1. Digital scholarship and literacy program | Investigate patron record management component of electronic reserves |
| 2. User-centered focus for services | Continue work of the ILL committee to enhance delivery and interlibrary loan work<br>Distribute to and inform staff of statistics for assessment of services by ILL and Circulation |
| 3. Enhancement of collections to support research, instruction, and service | Investigate collection statistics module of online catalog system |
| 4. Learning organization | Train branch libraries staff in the use of new technologies and software used in provision of ILL |
| 5. Library as place | Promote use of study rooms for student groups seeking a space for project work |
| 6. Diversify and leverage funding and resources | Collect all fees and fines available to the Library and leverage funding to maintain and enhance services and collections |

With this list in hand, Susan will work with the unit to add success measures and time frames to the goals. When these elements have been added, Susan will have an overall plan for the unit's work for the year.

## Planning a Day

In addition to planning the overall work of the unit, you also need to keep track of planning your own days and your own tasks. In his book *Getting Things Done,* David Allen suggests that each day there are three types of activities you might engage in: doing predefined work; doing work as it shows up; and defining your work.

### Predefined Work

If you are taking action on items from your "to do" list or your next-action list, you are doing predefined work. That is, you are working on tasks that you previously determined need to be worked on. These might include preparation for a meeting with a staff member, drafting performance evaluations, and making or returning phone calls.

### On-the-Spot Work

Some days it might seem as if you're not accomplishing anything from your list of tasks that need to be worked on because you have many interruptions. These interruptions, which are what Allen describes as "doing work as it shows up," involve anything that comes up unexpectedly: a staff member stops by to talk with you about a workflow problem, or your boss needs some budget figures for an emergency meeting the next morning. When you spend time on these interactions or tasks, you have prioritized these tasks, unconsciously or consciously, as more important than anything else you planned to do at that time on that day.

### Defining Your Work

Most library employees already spend time each day checking e-mail messages, reading paper mail, reading or writing meeting minutes, and responding to phone messages and voice mail. As a supervisor, you will add supervising staff and planning projects to this list. Some of these activities you will finish; many others will involve identifying action items or tasks that you will need to accomplish at some other time. These daily tasks, most of which are routine happenings each and every day for supervisors, are what Allen calls "defining your work." As you work your way through them, you will be adding items to your lists of tasks to accomplish.[2]

For example, it's late Friday afternoon and Susan is planning her work for the next week. She has three management meetings and a department meeting on her calendar, and she also has individual meetings with five of her staff. She also has two desk shifts. She examines her schedule to identify blocks of time when she can work on projects.

On her "to do" list she has three projects: prepare the unit's equipment requests, write two performance evaluations, and begin planning for a shift of part of the collection where it is becoming too crowded to shelve.

Next, she notes deadlines for the projects. The budget is due Tuesday, so she schedules a meeting with herself on Monday to ensure some uninterrupted time to work on the budget. The evaluations are due in two weeks, so Susan knows she can work on these as time permits. The collection shift will need to be done soon, so she wants to be sure that she has an outline of the process by the end of next week.

By identifying a few key projects that need to be done, and setting preliminary times to work on those projects, Susan has a good chance of getting the projects done. Without setting aside time for these projects, Susan could find her days taken up with daily tasks and interruptions that keep her from getting her own tasks done.

## Meeting Deadlines

Deadlines are a fact of life. Without them, most people would not accomplish very much. In your role of supervisor, you will work with staff to determine the appropriate steps to meet deadlines.

### Backwards-Planning Process

For projects with a fixed deadline, one planning technique is backwards-planning. With backwards-planning, you start with the deadline and plan backwards to the present time, developing a timetable listing the steps in the process. To do backwards-planning, you begin with the end event:

1. Make a list of tasks that must be accomplished before the deadline or event.
2. Working backwards with a calendar, start with the last step.

3. Write the last step on the calendar and note any tasks that need to be accomplished by specific dates to make the last step possible.
4. Repeat step 3 with the next-to-last step. Note related tasks.
5. Repeat step 4 with next steps until you reach the first step.
6. Determine deadlines for each step.
7. Delegate related tasks to appropriate staff.

Backwards-planning, with deadlines for each step and delegation of steps to appropriate people, will help to ensure that no important steps or components of the process are overlooked. Backwards-planning will also help all involved to know their roles and responsibilities and how much time it will take to complete the necessary tasks efficiently and effectively.

Projects where backwards-planning might be appropriate include an event that must happen on a certain day and where several staff members must participate in the project for it to be successful. For example, you are the cataloging supervisor and you learn that an upgrade to the cataloging module of your online catalog system is scheduled for the end of the year. Once the date of the upgrade has been determined, you can plan backwards from that date to make sure that everything is in place in time for the upgrade. Another example where backwards-planning could be effective is at the college library circulation desk. Each semester, your unit prepares for the first day of the new semester, when records for new library users will be added to the online system. This year everyone on campus will have a new ID card with a new identifying bar code. How much time do you have to make the necessary adjustments to routines? Who do you need to involve in the discussions? What other campus units use the bar code and for what data? Answering these questions will help you develop your backwards-planning outline.

Backwards-planning can also be used for smaller initiatives and for planning with staff members who work better when they have a structured workflow to follow.

## Organizing the Work of Others

As a unit head or supervisor, you will need to make decisions about how the work of your unit will be accomplished: what needs to be done and who will do it. As you will learn, most likely on your first day as a supervisor, each staff member is unique. Staff members have varying work styles and supervisors must understand, recognize, and accommodate the different work styles of the people they supervise. The good news is that while individuals exhibit unique traits, there are some similarities in work style preferences. Some employees prefer a great deal of structure; others find too much structure to be stifling. Depending on your own style, you may need to adjust the way that you work with individual staff members. (See chapter 4 on motivation and chapter 7 on diversity for more about different work styles.)

Work style preferences can be generalized into two groups: creative types and structured types. As a supervisor, you will observe very different behaviors from these groups, and may need to adjust your interactions with staff members of each type, depending on your own work style preference.

If you prefer a more structured environment, you may be frustrated when you supervise creative types even when the work is completed successfully. For example, creative staff members sometimes appear disorganized, yet often accomplish a great deal. To creative types, the more structural aspects of work life, such as routines or work guidelines, may seem too mundane to follow. On the other hand, your creative staff members will bring new ideas to stale routines, and if you let them, help you to rethink the work of your unit.

To support creative staff members and help them to be productive, you might adopt the following practices.

1. Present assignments in general terms, explaining the desired end result but allowing employees the latitude to find their own ways to that result. Establish timelines to keep productivity on track, but don't structure the work process.

2. Allow people to express risky ideas without immediately shooting them down. Criticizing these ideas or playing devil's advocate is the surest way to cut creative thinking off at the knees.

3. Let people work through their mistakes to find their own solutions, and allow them time for this as part of the creative process. It takes a lot of coal to make diamonds.

4. Learn how to praise someone's efforts without focusing on the result or product you want those efforts to generate.

5. Ask employees what you can do to provide a stimulating and supportive environment. You might be surprised at how simple some of their requests will be.

6. Sponsor workshops conducted by outside resources. Creative people are always looking to broaden the base of their knowledge and expertise. New faces bring fresh perspectives. Employees are sometimes more willing to question and raise issues with outsiders than they are with internal trainers or consultants.[3]

If you are a creative-type manager, supervising a staff member who wants, or even requires, structure can be frustrating. On the other hand, structured types are the people you want to help plan complex projects, as they are very skilled at breaking projects into logical steps. They are good at implementation as well, and after they understand what the work is and their role in the process, they will meet deadlines. Often their work spaces are neat and functional, and if necessary, someone else can easily step into their job.

To help you determine how best to work with a person who needs structure, you might adopt the following practices.

1. Start by laying out specific tasks and the small goals that must be accomplished by the end of the day. Be sure the employee has the necessary tools to complete the tasks, and knows how to use them.

2. Identify common problems that might arise, and establish a procedure for dealing with them. Some employees find it useful to have a chart or diagram that outlines priorities and procedures, while others might just take notes.

3. Meet with the employee at the end of the day to discuss how he or she approached the tasks and what actually got finished. Communication about expectations, and what worked and didn't work, is critical here.

4. Establish procedures for identifying and addressing emergencies and unexpected changes in priorities. At first, this might mean having the employee come to you whenever work deviates from the planned schedule. As the employee becomes more skilled in structuring and adjusting priorities, the procedures might shift to general guidelines for when to contact you and when to proceed without assistance.

5. Over time and as the employee's comfort with the structure progresses, designate daily tasks as part of the employee's routine, with the employee responsible for making them part of the workweek with less monitoring from the manager.

6. Be a good model. Show employees how you prioritize your day, and then ask them to tell you how they would in turn prioritize their own. Then compare the two, and show them how to make adjustments as needed.

7. Follow up to see what works and what doesn't, first on a daily and then on a less frequent (but no less than weekly) basis.[4]

## Time Management

Are you managing your time or is your time managing you? You may find that you ask yourself this question, as well as asking it of your staff. Much of what was discussed in the sections on setting objectives and meeting deadlines will help you to manage your time and the time of those who report to you. If reviewed regularly, calendars and action lists serve as effective time management tools for many people. Another technique, daily "to do" listing, is a universal of traditional time-management training.

Key points for successful "to do" listing include the following:

- Each and every day make a daily list of "to do" items. Make it a habit.
- Add items from previous days that need follow-up
- Prioritize tasks
- Batch similar tasks
- Keep "to do" readings on hand for when you have a few free moments
- At the end of the day, use today's "to do" list to write tomorrow's "to do" list[5]

Some management experts regard traditional "to do" lists as a waste of time. For example, David Allen prefers developing several lists, such as action lists, waiting-for lists, project lists, checklists, and someday/maybe lists.[6] You should determine the best system for yourself.

Other useful time management techniques include time analysis studies and group or team analysis.

A time analysis study can be as simple as jotting down your activities during your workday. The format could be a log or chart with an hour-by-hour record of the way you spend each day for a certain time period. (See figure 10-2.) Another option is to use your personal calendar to note all activities worked on during times when you don't have meetings scheduled. This second option works best when your calendar system allows plenty of room for notes. Keeping a log of your activity for a set time period, one week or one month, for example, can be very revealing.

Careful analysis of your personal time log will allow you to see how you are spending your time and whether that time was well spent. Questions you might ask include:

- Were you doing the right job at the right time?
- Could the job have been done at another time more effectively?
- Could you have delegated the job to someone else?
- What did you do that should not have been done at all?

**FIGURE 10-2 ■ Sample Time Analysis Log**

| Date: | | |
|---|---|---|
| *Time* | *Activity* | *Comments/Notes* |
| 8:00 a.m. | | |
| 8:15 a.m. | | |
| 8:30 a.m. | | |
| 8:45 a.m. | | |
| 9:00 a.m. | | |
| 9:15 a.m. | | |
| 9:30 a.m. | | |
| 9:45 a.m. | | |
| 10:00 a.m. | | |
| 10:15 a.m. | | |
| 10:30 a.m. | | |
| 10:45 a.m. | | |
| 11:00 a.m. | | |
| 11:15 a.m. | | |
| 11:30 a.m. | | |
| 11:45 a.m. | | |

You may notice a pattern to the interruptions in your day. How are you interrupted the most often? Are the interruptions mostly by telephone? Are they from staff, colleagues, or your boss dropping in to see you? How often do you check your e-mail? Even e-mail, with you controlling when and how often you check it, can be an interruption.

Consider the frequency of these interruptions. How important were the interruptions? How long did it take you to get back to the task you were working on? You can control, to a great extent, the nature and type of interruptions. For example, set aside time each day to go through your in-box and respond to e-mail messages. For some people, checking their e-mail once in the morning and once in the afternoon is adequate. Others may need to do so more frequently. Regardless of your situation, when you check your e-mail, look for urgent messages and tasks that you can finish in less than two minutes. Urgent messages, of course, should be dealt with right away. Quick tasks can be finished and the e-mails then deleted. Other e-mail messages, which require reading or action that will take more time, can be deferred to the block of time you set aside each day for e-mail. This simple change will save you significant time and keep your e-mail in-box better organized.

Another important exercise to help you manage your time, and the time of your staff, is a group or team time analysis. The purpose of this exercise is to focus on what the members of your unit or group do that affects the use of each other's time.

This exercise also requires a simple chart. To do the analysis, list all the people in your unit in the left-hand column. In the next two columns, note their actions, and other people's reactions to them. Note your actions. And in the right-hand column, note a plan to reduce time-wasting. (See figure 10-3.) A group or team analysis can be used to show how team members' actions both save and waste their colleagues' time.

**FIGURE 10-3 ■ Group Time Analysis**

| Staff Member | His or Her Action | Others' Reaction | Plan to Reduce Time-Wasting |
|---|---|---|---|
| Bob | Visits with others on the way to and from break | Stop working to visit | Encourage Bob to schedule break times with people he wants to visit with |
| Gina | Extended telephone conversations | Overhear personal information and are uncomfortable | Remind Gina to limit personal calls |
| Rhonda | Asks numerous staff the same work procedure questions | Give different details, become frustrated with all the questions | Schedule a set time for Rhonda to visit with her supervisor to ask questions |

## Conclusion

The key to a less-hectic work life is to organize, plan, and control your time. Annual plans begin with goals, objectives, and action plans with deadlines. Review progress regularly, at least quarterly. Monthly plans flow from the unit's action plans. Add regular activities such as budget preparation deadlines to your list of tasks and projects to be sure you meet your responsibilities. Weekly and daily plans help you keep focused on what needs to be done. Tasks are less likely to fall between the cracks when you keep action lists and "to do" lists.

Check off projects and tasks as you complete them. Celebrate the unit's completion of tasks and projects in order to thank staff for their hard work and to reinforce the benefits of planning. Work closely with your staff to develop systems that help them be productive, stay focused, and complete tasks and projects in a timely manner.

### NOTES

**1.** William Salmon, *The New Supervisor's Survival Manual* (New York: AMACOM, 1999), 78.

**2.** David Allen, *Getting Things Done: The Art of Stress-Free Productivity* (New York: Penguin, 2001), 50.

**3.** Gary McClain and Deborah S. Romaine, *The Everything Managing People Book* (Avon, Mass.: Adams Media, 2002), 93.

**4.** Allen, *Getting Things Done*, 97.

**5.** Mary Nofsinger, "Managing Work Time," in *Practical Help for New Supervisors,* ed. Joan Giesecke (Chicago: American Library Association, 1997), 83.

**6.** Allen, *Getting Things Done.*

# 11
# Managing Performance

**H**ave you ever enjoyed a performance evaluation conference? Have you received an evaluation that made you want to continue to do a good job? Or do you approach the annual evaluation session with the same reluctance many of us approach a visit to the dentist? Why do evaluations seem so painful? How can you as a supervisor create a process so that an annual performance appraisal is viewed as a positive event in your unit?

A good performance appraisal system begins with a clear understanding between the employee and the supervisor about the parameters of the job, the performance expectations, and an understanding of what will happen if performance standards are not met.[1] A clear job description with standards and expectations for each task is crucial. Clear expectations will help new employees understand what they need to do to succeed. Clear expectations also lay the foundation for any actions you may take to reward employees or to address performance concerns. Legally, you need to show that you are being consistent in defining, monitoring, and evaluating performance. Clear job descriptions and standards provide you with the road map you need to demonstrate consistency. Standards also protect both new supervisors and experienced managers from applying expectations in an arbitrary and subjective manner. Rewarding Mary and not John when both meet a given standard will lead to problems for you as their supervisor. At a minimum, you will be seen as inconsistent and can lose the respect of your unit. At the extreme, you may be guilty of discrimination and could face legal action.

Performance appraisal does not need to be a legal quagmire. Instead of approaching the issue of performance appraisal as an awful burden, try to see this aspect of management as an opportunity to work with your staff to make the unit excel. How can you do this?

## Standards and Expectations

One of the first steps in the process of establishing a positive performance appraisal system is to enlist the participation of your staff in setting standards and expectations. First, learn about your organization's standards and processes. Share these standards with the staff in your unit. Then work with each employee to determine how the standards will apply to their work. For example, if your organization has a standard in public service that no more than three legitimate customer complaints per year will be considered satisfactory, then discuss how you will assess a complaint. If a patron yells at a staff member at the desk because the staff member is following a policy the person does not like, as a supervisor, you may establish that this type of incident does not constitute a legitimate complaint. However, if the staff member yells back and uses foul language, it will be a legitimate complaint against the staffer. Outlining these types of expectations before an incident occurs will give you a foundation for rewarding positive behavior (staff did not yell) or addressing negative behavior (staff member did yell). If your organization does not have standards in place for a particular task or position, then you have the opportunity to develop or revise the standards with your staff. Including staff in the discussion will help them both understand and accept the standards you develop. The input from staff must be taken seriously. If you are only asking for input because you think you should, but you have no intention of using the staff input, staff will quickly become disillusioned and will see you as arbitrary rather than supportive.

Staff and managers may declare that quantitative expectations do not apply to their positions, that too much of what they do is subjective and cannot be measured. This argument often comes from the public service areas such as reference work or in describing supervisory roles. In these cases, more qualitative standards or outcomes may be needed. For example, for a fund-raising or public-relations position, the outcome of an encounter with a donor or with the media may be beyond the person's control. Nevertheless, expectations such as writing thank-you notes within seven days of a visit or interview will allow you as a supervisor to describe the behaviors the person does control and to evaluate those actions.

In larger organizations where a number of people perform similar tasks, developing standards and expectations helps to create organization-wide expectations. With generic standards in place, the organization is more likely to treat staff consistently among units. The more an organization can show that staff are treated consistently for similar work, the less opportunity there is for the organization to be found guilty of discrimination.

Generic standards should describe the duties and tasks, the expectations, and the impact of these standards. The standards should be understandable, clear, and meaningful.[2] For example, a generic statement of responsibility for supervisors may look like the following:

***Supervise the (Such-and-Such) Unit, consisting of (number) FTE (full-time equivalent) staff***

Work with the Human Resources Department to develop replacement ads for open positions.

Conduct job searches for vacant positions, including interviewing.

Make recommendations for hiring staff.

Establish performance expectations and develop position descriptions, reviewing and updating them annually or as needed.

Train staff or ensure that training occurs.

Evaluate progress and performance, offer support, and coach or mentor staff to meet library core competencies.

Meet regularly, both formally and informally, with staff.

Document performance issues.

Prepare written and oral evaluations of staff in the unit and conduct annual and probationary evaluations.

Recommend salary adjustments.

In consultation with supervisor and library administration, conduct disciplinary action or recommend termination for staff when necessary.

Follow all library personnel policies. Attend training programs offered by the Human Resources Department and the library to acquire an essential knowledge of personnel policies.

### *Impact statement*

Strong supervisory and management skills are vital for the smooth operation of the unit, for maintaining a welcoming environment for all staff, and for maintaining a positive library image with the public.

### *Plan and manage workflow of the unit, consisting of (number) FTE full-time staff and (number) FTE student assistants*

Develop unit goals and expectations in consultation with others as appropriate.

Develop and review policies and procedures. Recommend and execute changes as needed.

Create written documentation of routines and procedures.

Conduct unit meetings.

Schedule specific job duties, vacations, etc., for the unit.

Monitor unit staff time and attendance.

Delegate work.

Collect and analyze statistics.

Prepare the unit's annual report and other special reports as requested.

Serve as a resource person to resolve difficult and complex problems.

Serve as the contact person for other units and departments.

### *Impact statement*

Responses to and decisions about complex situations influence the library's effectiveness in local and national arenas.

The responsibilities listed above are required for a well-functioning and productive unit.

A generic statement of duties and expectations for a time and attendance clerk could look like the following:

### Time cards

Serve as time and attendance clerk for staff. Review time cards on a biweekly basis, checking for accuracy and completeness. Check for staff signature, total regular work hours and leave hours, enter correct payroll earnings codes, and sign off on time cards. Send all time cards to the library administration before the appropriate deadline.

Serve as time and attendance clerk for student assistants. Compare time cards against work schedule and bring any discrepancies to the attention of the supervisor. Check time cards for accuracy and completeness. Check for student signature, total the work hours, and sign student time cards. Enter student totals on student payroll sheet. Send all time cards and payroll sheets to the library administration before the appropriate deadline.

Maintain current knowledge of payroll and timekeeping procedures.

### Impact statement

Accuracy ensures that correct salary payments are made for hours worked and that time and attendance reporting is correct. Inaccurate reporting will violate library policies. Meeting deadlines allows the library administration to record payments and in turn allows the Payroll Office to process salary payments on time.

The challenge for you as a new supervisor is to be as specific as possible in writing standards, while not becoming so detailed that the person feels like a cog in a machine. Your staff need direction rather than step-by-step instructions that take away all need for them to think and contribute to the process of planning the workflow.

Standards and expectations should be reviewed annually to be sure they are still relevant to the work and the unit. A change in a software program can result in a change in workflow that then affects expectations. Unless the expectations are reviewed regularly, they tend to become less applicable as the environment changes.

## Performance Evaluation Systems

Once job descriptions and standards and expectations are in place, you have the beginning of a performance evaluation system. Don't put these documents away only to drag them out in a year to see how staff are doing. Instead, these are documents you need to work with and refer to throughout the year. First, verify that the staff are clear about job duties and expectations. For new employees, you need to review this information in the orientation process. Then follow up with employees every few months to be sure they understand how the expectations apply to their positions. In some organizations, the human resources manager will schedule a ninety-day review with each new employee to review the expectations and be sure the employee understands the job. Having someone outside the unit do this review can help unearth misunderstandings that the supervisor might miss. For all employees, standards and expectations should be reviewed semiannually, both to ensure that changes in performance are addressed early and to ensure that any changes in expectations that may be needed are handled quickly.

It is very important that the supervisor clearly communicate changes in policies and procedures as these changes occur. Do not wait for a formal performance review to tell a staff member that the organization's policy has changed.

It is not fair to hold an employee accountable for failing to follow a change in policy or procedure if that change has not been clearly communicated to the staff. Sending out a written notice of the change may not be sufficient to guarantee that all employees are fully aware of it. Reviewing changes at a department or unit meeting may be more effective because it will allow employees to ask questions about the changes. This way both the supervisor and the employees can be sure they understand the changes, understand why they have occurred, and have reviewed how the changes affect the unit.[3]

## *Ongoing Discussion*

Discussing job performance can be built into a regular routine with each staff member so that you are keeping communication lines open in your unit. A supervisor should have a meeting every two to four weeks with each staff member to review how the job is going, answer any questions that have arisen, and ensure that, as a supervisor, you know how your staff are doing. These meetings can be informal in tone, but should always give the staff member a chance to report progress and discuss issues. They are also a time when, as a supervisor, you can address any questions or concerns you have. With regular meetings, you can avoid unpleasant surprises and can help staff members stay on course. These meetings are also a time to recognize good work, praise staff for successes, and reach agreement on new projects or objectives.

## Annual Performance Appraisal

Most organizations will have a system for annual performance evaluations. The process may include a standardized form and a numerical rating system, or the system may use open-ended letters, leaving the process up to the supervisor. No matter what system you use, a good supervisor will write a clear analysis of the staff member's performance. Vague statements that read like a horoscope will not be helpful to the staff member, nor will they provide the employee with any advice on what is working well. You should present a balanced view of the staff member's performance, noting strengths and accomplishments. Emphasizing strengths will help a staff member focus on successes and help provide a more motivating environment. A performance evaluation is also a means to document any concerns about a person's performance. Again, balance is a key. Do not overemphasize recent experiences or ignore past events. The evaluation should reflect the entire year.

To complete a successful performance evaluation, follow these steps.[4]

1. Review the staff member's job description and standards and expectations. Be sure you know what the employee is supposed to be doing.

2. Review your notes on the employee's performance for the year. Identify major successes and areas of outstanding performance. Note, too, any areas that need improvement.

3. Complete the evaluation form or write the evaluation letter. Be sure to focus on the current year's performance. Note improvements from the last evaluation. Do not raise past issues that have been resolved more than a year ago. Tie performance to expectations so that the staff member knows how the work he or she has done is reflected in the evaluation.

4. The evaluation should contain no surprises. If you have not already addressed a problem this year, you should not blame the staff member for not improving. You may list this as an area for growth, but it should not adversely affect a staff member's overall rating.

5. Once the form is complete, give it to the staff member to review prior to any discussion about performance. Some organizations will specify how many workdays the staff member has to review a written evaluation prior to an oral conference. Carefully follow your organization's procedures.

6. Plan the oral conference. Do not read the written form to the employee. Rather, decide on strengths to highlight, accomplishments to review, and concerns to discuss.

7. At the oral conference, outline the employee's strengths and note areas of improvement. Answer any questions the staff member may have. Listen carefully to his or her concerns. Be sure to address any uncertainty, disagreements, or confusion.

8. Review any concerns you have about the employee's performance. Discuss plans to address these concerns.

9. Discuss goals and objectives for the coming year. Include plans to address concerns, but also include ways to build on the staff member's strengths to improve performance and reach excellence.

10. Close the conference by signing forms as needed. Review any follow-up that is planned.

11. Since performance evaluations are confidential personnel papers, be sure to file the forms as outlined in your organization's procedures immediately after the oral conference. Do not carelessly leave evaluation forms lying around your office. You must keep them safe.

Once the conference is completed and the forms are safely processed, do not ignore performance issues for a year. Do follow-up as needed. Meet regularly with your staff, discuss their accomplishments, and review areas for growth.

## Performance Problems

When issues of performance do arise, you need to address them quickly. For example, explaining to a staff member that they missed a field on a cataloging record or were late to a desk shift is more meaningful closer to the event so you are both clear about the actions that were taken. Leaving discussions of concerns about behavior for too long means that both the staff member and you will be less clear about the details of the issue in question.

Although you should address issues as they arise, you also need to take a moment to plan your conversation with the staff member. It is never appropriate to yell at a staff member, whether in the presence of others or not, unless the person is doing something that is hazardous or dangerous to themselves or others.

To address a performance issue, you should take the following steps.[5]

1. First, clarify in your own mind the behavior or performance you want to see from the staff member. Review the standards and expectations for the

task in question so you can assess the situation as objectively as possible.

2. Gather facts about the staff member's performance. For example, if attendance is an issue, know how many times the person was late and how that number compares to the standards and expectations.

3. Analyze the facts to determine if the problem can be prevented, if the employee has enough information to do the task, or if the task is too large for one person to do. For example, if you have not trained a staff member to select vendors for ordering books, you cannot fault the person if he or she does not make choices that are appropriate.

4. Set up a meeting with the employee and develop an outline of what you want to accomplish. Be sure you are clear about the behavioral or performance issues you want to address. Have examples and documentation handy so you can be as objective and clear as possible.

5. Hold the meeting with the staff member. Outline your concerns using the facts you have gathered. Be clear but not cruel. You can tell someone they were late three days out of five without being insulting.

6. Ask the employee for his or her perspective. How does the staff member think he or she is doing? Does the person acknowledge the problem? Does the person understand the task and how to accomplish the work?

7. With the staff member, develop a plan for improvement. Reach agreement on what changes will be needed to resolve the problem. Set a date to follow up on the issue and review progress.

8. Hold a follow-up session. Has the behavior improved? Are expectations being met? If performance has improved, you and the staff member have been successful in addressing the problem. Monitor the work as you would for any other staff member to be sure that performance remains satisfactory.

What do you do if the staff member's performance has not improved? How can you address continued performance issues without getting discouraged? First, find out about your organization's procedure for progressive discipline. Most organizations will have a step-by-step process for you to follow. Usually, the process begins with giving an oral warning to the employee about the problem. Oddly enough, you need to document when you have this conversation and be sure the employee knows the conversation is an oral warning. If a person is coming in late, telling the person they need to watch their attendance and not giving specifics will not be sufficient to serve as the beginning of a disciplinary process. You need to be clear about what is expected and what will happen if the performance does not improve.

The next step is a written warning. Here you document the problem and provide a written copy to the staff member. Develop a time frame for addressing the problem and outline the next steps if the employee's performance does not improve.

Meet regularly with the employee to review his or her progress. Employees having problems will need guidance and attention from you to be sure they know when they are making progress. You also need to document a lack of change so that you have enough information to move to the next steps in the process.

If all else fails, you may ultimately recommend that an employee be terminated. If you are reaching this point of the disciplinary process, be sure you work with your organization's human resources office, your supervisor, and any union representatives that are part of the process.

## Firing an Employee

When a staff member does not meet expectations or is not doing the job you need done, and you have documented your efforts to correct the problem, you need to recommend that the person be terminated. While it is not pleasant to have to fire someone, it is also not healthy for the unit if you tolerate poor performance. When you do tolerate poor performance, you force others in the unit to do the work of the inadequate staff member. This will build resentment toward you and you can lose the respect of your entire unit.

Firing an employee, though, takes careful planning.[6] You want to be sure you have followed all of your organization's policies and procedures, reviewed any pertinent labor agreements, and alerted appropriate officials to the situation. Pick a time to meet with the employee. Many superiors will plan the meeting for the end of the day so the employee can leave the workplace at the end of the meeting.

Because terminating a staff member can be an emotional encounter, you want to be sure you have arranged a secure, safe location for the meeting. Determine if security is needed and if so, have someone available during the meeting. The night before, be sure that all computer work the person has been doing is backed up. Arrange to have passwords and access codes changed as the meeting concludes. You need to protect the unit and the organization should the employee try to harm the organization.

The meeting with the employee can include your supervisor or a representative from your organization's human resources department. Be sure to have at least one person with you to help document the meeting and help keep the meeting under control.

## At the Meeting

The meeting itself consists of the following steps.

1. Briefly review the problems. Do not go into great detail, since you don't want to prolong the meeting or make the employee feel any worse than needed.

2. Briefly review the steps taken to address the problem.

3. Tell the person that they are being terminated, what pay if any they will receive, and how to get their personal items out of the office. Be as specific as you can about these arrangements and still be brief.

For example, if a staff member named Mary has failed to maintain a schedule, the meeting might go as follows. You say, "Mary, you and I have met eight times over the past two months to discuss your schedule. You are expected to be at work by 8:30 a.m. You have been arriving 15–30 minutes late over 75 percent of the time. Since you have failed to meet expectations and have been unable to correct the problem, we are notifying you that today is your last day of work. You will receive two weeks' severance pay. Tom, our human resources person, will accompany you to your desk so you can pack up your things and leave."

Mary may become emotional, may declare the process is unfair, or may hardly react at all. You should be careful not to debate the process with Mary and to stay as calm as possible. Once Mary has regained her composure, have someone escort her to her desk and help her pack. Conversely, you may make arrangements for Mary to clean out her desk after work hours. In any case, follow your organization's routine and procedures for these situations.

Remember, this meeting is not about you. You should avoid telling the staff member how bad you feel or how hard it is for you to fire someone. The staff member is unlikely to care how you feel and could resent you for focusing on your own feelings instead of the staff member's situation. Be empathetic and professional as you conduct the meeting.

While firing someone is an unpleasant task for a supervisor, if you have followed the organization's procedures, tried to work with the staff member, and been clear about the consequences of not meeting expectations, you will know that you tried your best to resolve the issue.

When performance is a regular topic of discussion, it becomes less burdensome to you and to the staff member. The discussion becomes a way to build on performance and to encourage staff growth. The annual evaluation becomes a time to reflect on past accomplishments and plan future direction. When an evaluation is part of an ongoing disciplinary process, such discussions may not seem like fun, but they will not be as burdensome as you may have feared they would be.

## Conclusion

Performance appraisal begins with a clear job description and understandable standards and expectations. Performance discussions should be an ongoing part of your regular communication with your staff. Address issues quickly. Give praise and recognition regularly. Annual performance appraisals can be a productive time to discuss goals and objectives. They don't need to be a painful, burdensome process. While terminating an employee can be painful, if you carefully follow your organization's rules and procedures, you can make the process less difficult for everyone involved.

### NOTES

**1.** Gary McClain and Deborah S. Romaine, *The Everything Managing People Book* (Avon, Mass.: Adams Media, 2002), 177.

**2.** The generic statements of responsibility are adapted from the University of Nebraska-Lincoln Libraries, NU Values generic statements, 2003.

**3.** Joan Giesecke, ed., *Practical Help for New Supervisors* (Chicago: American Library Association, 1997), 26–27.

**4.** Ibid., 30–31.

**5.** Ibid., 27–29.

**6.** McClain and Romaine, *Everything Managing People Book,* 177.

# 12
# Managing Meetings

As a supervisor, you will attend many meetings. In fact, there may be days when you question whether you ever do anything but attend meetings. It has been estimated that many supervisors spend at least one-third to one-half of their work time in meetings.[1] Often you will chair or lead meetings in your role as a supervisor. While chairing meetings can sometimes seem like a daunting task, the skills for effective meeting management can be learned.

You will participate in many different types of meetings. Some of your meetings will be regularly scheduled sessions with individual staff members. You may also lead department or unit meetings. Some meetings will be called to address specific topics. Others may be open-ended sessions, with the intent to brainstorm ideas about future directions. The skills necessary for effective meeting management can apply to many if not all types of meetings, and once you have learned them you will be ready to lead productive meetings.

## The Basics of Meetings

There are some key points that apply to any meeting.

*Meetings should have a purpose.* First, be sure you have a reason to meet. Don't waste people's time by holding a meeting that has no purpose.

*Begin meetings on time.* We all have busy lives. Starting and ending meetings on time will signal that you value the time of the people at the meetings.

*Few meetings should last longer than one hour.* Try to keep most meetings to one or two hours. Meetings that go longer may become repetitive instead of constructive.

*Develop and share agendas prior to meetings.* Agendas alert participants to the topics to be covered and give participants time to prepare for meaningful discussion.

## Meetings with Individual Staff Members

For supervisors new to an organization, or new to a supervisory role, initial orientation meetings with every member of the unit are particularly important, since they help to set the tone for your work with the unit. A set list of questions to be asked of each member serves as your agenda for the meetings. While it is not necessary to rigidly follow the list of questions, you should try to cover as many of them as possible. First of all, you need the information the answers will give you, and second, staff members will likely compare notes about the meetings. At the initial orientation meeting, it is important to keep the discussion to work-related topics. By asking everyone the same questions, you will be seen as a fair and impartial supervisor, interested in the opinions and viewpoints of all. Questions you may want to ask include:

What are the person's areas of responsibility?

What are the person's top priorities?

Does the person have problems or concerns you should know about?

What are the person's expectations?

How satisfied is the person with the way the department is currently running?

What is the workload? Is it reasonable?

Are there areas of interest that the person would like to pursue?

How satisfied is the person with his or her current position?

Is the position description up-to-date?

If the person supervises others, does he or she have concerns about any employees?

Do people have the right equipment and skills to do their jobs?

What resources is the person responsible for?

What other departments does the person work for?

Does the person have concerns about other departments or units that as a manager you should be aware of?

What is the person's view of the organization's goals and objectives?

What are the person's career plans?

What changes would the person recommend be considered?

What else do you as manager need to know about the person, the department, or the organization?[2]

Staff members' answers to these questions will help you to develop an understanding of your unit.

After the initial orientation meetings with staff, you will want to plan for regular meetings with staff members who report directly to you. These meetings will help you stay up-to-date with the work of your unit, allow you to develop good working relationships with staff, and provide early indications of both successes and failures. As you learn more about your staff members, you will be in a better position to assess not only their skills, knowledge, and competencies at performance evaluation time, but also their unique talents that may be instrumental in moving the work of your unit forward.

Individual staff meetings should take place as frequently as necessary to provide you with enough information to know that a staff member is accomplishing his or her work. Depending on your proximity to staff work-stations, you may be able to informally assess staff progress and may find it necessary to meet formally less frequently. In some situations, though, it may be necessary to meet weekly or biweekly. And, as addressed in chapter 11 on performance appraisal, addressing and handling performance problems will take additional meetings.

## Unit or Department Meetings

Once you have oriented yourself to the unit and learned more about its culture, it will be much easier to lead unit meetings. While scheduling regular meetings for your unit is important, the necessary frequency of these meetings will vary for several reasons, including the size of your unit, the unit's place in the larger organizational structure, and simply the mechanics of arranging a meeting.

If the unit is small, with fewer than five individuals, frequent formal meetings may be unnecessary, particularly if your work areas are situated near each other and the unit has a culture of close communication and collaboration. Unit members may be in close contact with you and with each other and will need communication solely about events and issues pertaining to the larger organization.

Whether large or small in staff size, any unit that is part of a large organization will need regular communication about that organization, and meetings are an effective way to share this information. E-mail has made it much easier to share news, particularly for large organizations. However, as a supervisor, you are responsible for communicating news to staff, and regularly scheduled meetings are an effective way to do this. Unit meetings provide an opportunity for two-way communication: overall organization to unit and vice versa.

For some units, the nature of the work completed by the unit may help determine the frequency of the meetings. In an environment of quickly changing priorities, frequent meetings are crucial. For a unit embarking on a new project or program, regularly scheduled meetings are necessary for planning purposes and to stay on target. Finding a regular meeting time can be a challenge for all supervisors, whether they supervise public service operations or behind-the-scenes technical services or systems staff. Supervisors of public service operations, where desks are open and staffed all hours that the library is open, may find it very difficult to schedule a meeting time that works for all staff members. In these situations, a supervisor may need to rely on student workers or assistants to staff desks. Another alternative is for a supervisor to lead the same meeting twice. (While this does allow for 100 percent participation, it may also lead to miscommunication.) The staff in units such as technical services or automated systems departments may have more flexible schedules and alternate work sites. While it may be difficult to plan a unit meeting at least once a month, your job of supervisor will be easier if you can accomplish this.

## Preparation for Meetings

Effective meeting preparation is the key for all meetings. As a supervisor, you will often be in a position to determine or define the purpose of the meeting.

### *Meetings for Information Dissemination*

For some meetings, the purpose may be simply to communicate news and directives from the larger organization. These meetings are sometimes called "information and briefing meetings."[3] For example, you may schedule meetings with your unit to relay information from a larger departmental or organizational meeting you have attended. The purpose of the meeting is to communicate these organizational issues to your unit. Distributing an agenda prior to the meeting, with basic details about the content of the meeting, will convey your purpose for meeting to participants.

### *Planning, Problem-Solving, and Other Issue-Driven Meetings*

You may schedule meetings for other purposes than simply communicating with unit members. Meetings can be for planning purposes for an upcoming project or initiative, problem-solving sessions for new workflow routines, or even decision-making meetings where reaching consensus through group discussion is a necessary function.

For special topic-driven meetings, you will be most successful if you state the meeting's objectives and expectations prior to the meeting. As with regular information and briefing meetings, topic-driven meetings should include an agenda, which should be distributed to all participants prior to the meeting. The agenda can be quite simple or very detailed, depending on the topic and type of the meeting, although it will most often be more detailed than the agenda for a regularly scheduled unit meeting.

The following is a sample agenda for a meeting.

[bcc: all library staff]

The Executive Committee will meet on Tuesday, March 16, at 9:00 a.m. in the library conference room.

*Agenda:*

1. Approval of minutes from the 3/2/04 Exec meeting.
2. Libraries depository/retrieval facility update
3. Review of revised computer rotation
4. Review of hours
5. Review of paper distribution of Exec minutes
6. Student assistant budgets—reminder of year-end spending
7. Quarterly projects
8. Other
9. Announcements

Other important steps to plan for a meeting include choosing an appropriate time and location for it and arranging the meeting room in an appropriate manner to allow all to participate. For many smaller group meetings, a circle or square will be most conducive to active participation. For larger meetings, it may be necessary to use a different seating arrangement.

The last step in meeting preparation is to be certain that all participants, the staff you supervise, know where and when the meeting will take place. Having regularly scheduled meetings in regular locations takes away the guesswork for staff, so they can plan their work and manage their time accordingly.

## Conducting the Meeting

At the beginning of the meeting, greet the staff and help them to feel welcome. Make sure that staff members with special needs have appropriate accommodations. For example, a hearing-impaired staffer may need to sit directly in front of you if he or she reads lips, and a staffer with mobility concerns may need greater aisle width. These issues should be considered prior to the meeting when you are determining the meeting room and furniture layout.

Start on time. Through careful attention to the agenda, you will be able to accomplish much during your meeting. Encourage discussion and feedback and keep the conversation on topic. Keep notes during the meeting so that you will be able to write minutes and distribute them to participants and possibly to your supervisor as well. At the conclusion of the meeting, summarize key points, repeat action items and individuals' responsibilities, and set a date, time, and place for the next meeting. And finally, end on time.

## Skills for Handling Problem Behaviors during Meetings

Sometimes meetings just don't go well despite your best intentions and attention to all of the pre-meeting details. The reasons might include, for example, participants who don't want to participate, someone with a hidden agenda, the wrong people "at the table," or perhaps a lack of leadership manifesting itself in a meeting that seems out of control. There are several communication strategies that you, as meeting leader, can use to help meetings flow smoothly and be successful. These techniques include active listening, clarification, summarizing, acknowledging the intensity of feelings or emotions, reframing, and the use of "I" statements.

### Active Listening

To listen actively, you convey interest in what you are hearing, restate the speaker's ideas, reflect the speaker's feelings, and then summarize what you have heard.

"So, you are saying that the new organizational structure is troubling you. I can see why you might feel worried about your place in the new department. Let's talk more about . . ."

### Clarification

You can use open-ended questions to clarify what you are hearing. This will help you to learn more about the situation and to begin to identify issues. An open-ended question might begin with the words, "Tell me more about . . ." With clarification, it is important to focus on the issues, not the person or personality who is speaking. Be careful not to imply judgment in your questions. Try to find something of value in everything that is said.

### Summarizing

Summarizing allows you to pull together all of the facts before moving on in your discussion. This helps to clarify what has been said and agreed to.

It also allows the group to reach consensus and move forward or to recognize that more discussion is needed.

"Before we move on, let me review what I think we've decided so far. We agreed to start the new process on February 1. Joe and Jim will work together to update our policy documents. Jerry will work with the systems office to load the new software on our computers. I will alert the other departments that February 1 is the start date. We agreed to meet once each week until February. And, finally, we will assess how the new process is working on February 15. Does that cover all the details we discussed?"

### *Dealing with Emotions*

It is important to recognize that sometimes feelings and emotions are an integral part of the message being conveyed. Acknowledging the intensity of those feelings can be helpful in understanding and resolving an issue. Acknowledging and paraphrasing, and reframing, are two communication techniques that can help with emotional messages. Reframing neutralizes the messages, making them more acceptable to the listener. Reframing can be used to increase or decrease the emotional level, and if necessary, to remove the emotion from the content.

For example, if you hear, "There is no way we can possibly pull this off by the end of the month," you might reframe it to say, "So, you think this won't work. Why won't it?"

If you hear, "He never listens to me," you might reframe it to, "It sounds like you're frustrated with Joe."

These reframed comments will encourage the speaker to reply, possibly providing you with more information or insight into the problem. Reframing separates the person from the problem.

Acknowledging and paraphrasing is an active listening technique that allows you to let the staff person know that you've heard what he or she said, that you understand the intensity of his or her feelings, and that having those feelings is okay. This technique can be difficult to master. Stating that you understand the staff member, or their problem, is not necessarily acknowledging it. There are situations in which you will not want to recognize the emotional aspect of the message. For example, your department is discussing a new work schedule which requires that more staff arrive at 7:00 a.m. to work on a computer upgrade. Mary, an older employee, is frustrated with Joe, a younger employee, who is always late for these early morning projects. "You cannot trust him to show up," she says.

Now is not the time to acknowledge Mary's emotion. Instead, try summarizing the issue and ask the group how they can be sure everyone arrives on time to help. In these situations, it will be more effective if you use another communication technique, such as reframing or summarizing, rather than acknowledging and paraphrasing.

### "I" Statements

"I" statements are used to describe your feelings, describe someone's behavior in neutral, descriptive terms, and describe the results of the behavior. In positive situations, for example, when you are telling a staff member how much you appreciate their work, "I" statements can be very powerful motivating messages.

"I am so pleased . . . when you jump in to help plan new projects . . . because I value your opinion and experience."

"I am so glad . . . you came to the meeting and participated . . . because I know how important this issue is to you."

In negative situations, "I" statements are useful because you can convey how strongly you feel about the situation.

"I feel frustrated . . . when you forget to close out the cash register . . . because I know you are aware of the library's policy."

"I am frustrated . . . when you don't participate at meetings . . . because I know you have valuable input to share."

## After the Meeting

### Minutes

As soon as possible after the meeting, write and distribute your notes or minutes on it, preferably within a few days. For regular meetings with individual staff members, writing summary notes about the meeting will help you to keep track of the employee's performance. You can follow up on particular issues raised at these meetings, note when to revisit a particular topic, and in general keep track of the employee's progress. Notes from the meetings can be shared with the staff member, to ensure that you and the staffer have a shared understanding of the discussion at the meeting. Notes from meetings with individual staff members can also be helpful for performance evaluation purposes, both for noting the accomplishments of a high-performing individual, and for the paperwork necessary when corrective action must be taken.

For unit or department meetings, minutes help keep all staff, whether or not they attended the meeting, on track and informed. The minutes should include points raised at the meeting, key components of discussions, decisions that were made, decisions that still need to be made, tasks to be performed, staff responsible for those tasks, next steps, and so on. Distributing the meeting minutes promptly is important, both for you as a supervisor so that you can manage the activities and work of your unit, but also for staff members who may need reminders about the activities taking place in the unit or organization and their own role in the process. As the supervisor, you are responsible for the necessary follow-up to the meeting. You make sure that staff understand their responsibilities and carry them out.

The following are sample minutes from an executive committee or library management group meeting. Only action items, decisions, and key updates are included in the minutes.

---

### Sample Minutes from the Executive Committee Agenda

Executive Committee Minutes No. 201                                   March 16

1. *Minutes*

   The minutes to the March 2 Executive Committee meeting were approved.

2. *Libraries Depository/Retrieval Facility Update*

   Bids for the LDRF will likely go out mid- to late April. Librarians are working on selection of titles in preparation for closing the three branches. Initial selections are due May 1.

3. *Revised Computer Rotation*

   Executive Committee approved the updated computer rotation schedule.

4. *Hours*

   Library hours were reviewed. Based on patron usage counts, the current hours schedule will remain effective for the next year.

5. *Distribution of Exec Minutes*

   Executive Committee minutes will be distributed electronically only.

6. *Student Assistant Budgets*

   E-mail the Director's Office by March 23 if you have student assistant money that you will not be using this fiscal year.

7. *Quarterly Projects*

   Technical Services' proposed projects for April–June were approved.

8. *Announcements*

   The next Executive Committee meeting will be April 6.

## Follow-up after Meetings

For meetings where your purpose was to gather input or brainstorm ideas, it is critical that you relay to individuals who participated in the meeting the decisions made and the results of the meeting. You should explain why you have decided whatever you have decided and why some ideas or suggestions that were raised cannot be implemented at this time. This will help staff to realize that their participation and input are valued, and that while you cannot implement all of their ideas all of the time, you appreciate their time, effort, and creativity.

## Benefits of Meetings

Meetings provide a mechanism for sharing information, decision-making, problem-solving, idea generation or brainstorming, and team-building, to name just a few of the benefits. With the increasing use of e-mail in libraries for communication purposes, it may be tempting to forgo scheduling at least some meetings with staff. While it is not a good idea to meet just for the sake of meeting, meetings do indicate to your staff that you value their input and contributions to the unit and organization, and that you find meeting with them in person to be useful in your management of the unit. Take care to consider carefully whether meeting in person is appropriate and necessary. If there is a clear need, schedule the meeting. If not, an alternative to a group meeting that will take care of the issue may be more appropriate.

## Conclusion

In conclusion, keep in mind the following basic tenets of good meetings.

> As the meeting leader, you will:
>> distribute the agenda in advance
>> set goals and discussion time limits for each agenda item
>> start on time
>> stay on task
>> end on time
>> disseminate minutes in a timely manner
>
> As leader, you encourage all participants to:
>> come to the meeting prepared

remember that only one person speaks at a time
participate, but do not dominate
respect differences
expect differences
disagree in a respectful manner

## NOTES

**1.** Myrna J. McCallister and Thomas H. Patterson, "Conducting Effective Meetings," in *Practical Help for New Supervisors,* ed. Joan Giesecke (Chicago: American Library Association, 1997), 58.

**2.** Joan Giesecke, *Practical Strategies for Library Managers* (Chicago: American Library Association, 2001), 34–35.

**3.** Barbara I. Dewey and Sheila D. Creth, *Team Power: Making Library Meetings Work* (Chicago: American Library Association, 1993), 28.

# 13
# Managing Rewards

**F**inding ways to reward employees beyond the traditional structure of salaries and wages has never been easy. Sometimes library budgets are determined by the larger organization (college or university, school board, library board, etc.) and supervisors may have little control over how extra funds are determined and distributed.

## Salaries and Monetary Incentives

Policies for how salaries are distributed may be determined outside of the library, may be a part of a union contract, or may be part of an overall organizational system. As a supervisor, you will want to know if employees are rewarded for performance in the form of merit increases, if raises are automatic (as in cost-of-living increases), or if they are based on seniority. If performance is the basis for merit increases, then be sure you are conducting appropriate performance appraisals, documenting good performance as well as performance problems. Be fair to your staff by ensuring that you follow organizational rules in performance procedures, so that your staff will qualify for and be recognized with merit salary increases.

Salary increases alone are not sufficient as the only monetary rewards and incentives for encouraging and celebrating good performance. As a supervisor, you will want to explore what other options you have for recognizing outstanding performance, celebrating success, and encouraging each employee to do the best he or she can.

Some libraries will have reward structures, incentives, or bonus plans and awards already in place. Check to see if your library has policies on rewarding employees. An example of a library incentive plan is found in figure 13-1.

FIGURE 13-1 ■ Incentive Award Policy

### The Guiding Principles of Incentive Awards for the University Libraries
University of Nebraska-Lincoln
October 1999

Link Incentive Awards to the Libraries' mission and goals. Incentive Award decisions must support the University Libraries' goals and values.

Base on prospective or future performance. Incentive Awards are given for prospective work and reward objective, measurable outcomes.

Provide equity in the distribution of Incentive Awards. All regular employees in the Office/Service and Managerial/Professional classifications should be given equal opportunity to be rewarded for the results of their work. Faculty members are not eligible to receive Incentive Awards.

Give Incentive Awards for specific achievements. Actions that produce positive results, rather than subjective feelings and visibility, should be rewarded.

Hold supervisors accountable for using Incentive Awards to achieve or recognize results. Employees feel strongly that supervisors should be responsible for ensuring recognition is linked to positive actions and contributions.

Give Incentive Awards in a timely manner. Employees feel that recognition given in a timely manner is most effective.

Encourage both individual and group Incentive Awards. Group awards encourage teamwork and foster the cooperation needed to address the many complex issues faced by the Libraries.

Give employees a choice in the type of Incentive Award. Whenever possible, recipients should be allowed a choice in the type of award they receive.

Publicize Incentive Awards. The libraries must be open in publicizing who receives Incentive Awards.

Provide flexibility for Incentive Award programs at the department level.

Provide training for supervisors and staff in effective use of Incentive Awards. A discussion of the recognition process should be included with training for new supervisors.

Periodically monitor and evaluate the Incentive Award program. Report and keep statistics on an annual basis.

Incentive Award programs are subject to change or discontinuation at the option of the University Libraries and/or the University of Nebraska–Lincoln.

Remember that for any reward to be successful, you want to be sure it is tied to performance. You will find that you see the behaviors you reward. Be sure you reward the behaviors which you want to see in your unit.

Review the award options that exist and remember to nominate your staff for them when appropriate. Even if your staff do not win, staff members will be pleased that you took the initiative to submit a nomination for them.

## Nonmonetary Rewards

In times of tight budgets or budget cuts, rewarding employees with monetary awards may not be possible. When funding is an issue, consider nonmonetary rewards.

There are many examples of nonmonetary rewards that you can use to recognize your employees. Not all rewards will fit with your organization. Look for rewards that blend well with your library's policies and your unit's culture. Nonmonetary rewards can include such things as flexible scheduling, job design, celebrations, and awards.[1]

*Flexible scheduling.* Flexible scheduling allows employees to plan their work schedules around other factors in their lives. With many libraries open more than forty hours per week, staff may have a variety of options available to them to schedule their workweek. When these options are available, work with your staff members to find schedules that match both their needs and the unit's needs. Finding a schedule that works for you, a staff member, and your unit can help a staff member feel valued and be more productive.

*Job design.* Job enrichment, job sharing, and job rotation are all options you can use to give an employee new challenges and help the person learn new skills. In job enrichment, a staff member may take on new responsibilities or special projects. These challenges may be assigned as recognition of outstanding performance on the basic job tasks. In job rotation, staff may exchange positions for a limited time to have the opportunity to try new tasks. In job sharing, two staff may share a position or set up tasks so that they have time to handle other duties or work part-time. In reviewing job design options, be sure you offer opportunities fairly to your staff and do not show favoritism. Everyone who is performing well should have an opportunity to try these different task options.

*Celebrations.* One way to recognize outstanding performance is to celebrate successes. Celebrations can vary from elaborate recognition ceremonies to a quick unit coffee break to say thank-you to a staff member or team. While formal events provide a more structured approach that recognizes unusual efforts, quick celebrations help the staff understand that outstanding effort will be recognized.

*Awards.* Many libraries have annual recognition awards to acknowledge staff excellence. These awards highlight the accomplishments of staff throughout the year and over time. Learn the criteria for these awards and share them with your staff so they can see how they can qualify for these recognitions.

Within the unit, you and your staff can create ways to recognize each other's work. Giving awards for new ideas, for suggestions that improve workflow, or for ideas that save money are just a few ways you can show staff that you value their efforts.

Be sure that you don't overuse awards. You want to promote and recognize desired behaviors and be sure that the performance warrants a reward, not try to give everyone an award every month.

Figure 13-2 lists the various options for nonmonetary rewards.

**FIGURE 13-2 ■ Noncash Incentives**

| | |
|---|---|
| Time off with pay (1 to 40 hours) | Flexible scheduling (flextime, flexitour, variable day, variable week, etc.) |
| Tickets to local performance (may include movie, theatre, sports event, etc.) | Job design (job rotation and job enrichment or enlargement) |
| Gift certificates | Celebrations of milestones on the job |
| Computer accessories, software, or equipment | Providing desirable committee appointments or related assignments |
| Office equipment | Asking the employee to represent the library at professional functions |
| Professional development funds | Asking the employee to accompany you to appropriate business meetings |
| Parking permit for one year | |
| Campus recreation membership | |
| Other choices to be determined by the employee, supervisor, and library director | Extending an invitation to coauthor a publication or work jointly on a special initiative |

## Generational Issues and Rewards

Changes in the demographics of the workforce complicate the reward structure. Traditional rewards no longer motivate all employees. Recognizing and understanding generational differences may help you, in your supervisory role, to provide meaningful monetary and nonmonetary rewards for employees.

Writers and researchers on multigenerational differences have varying opinions on the number of generations currently living and the characteristics that distinguish them. The generation of people born before 1924, age 80 or older in 2004 and largely not members of the current workforce, are often called matures. The veterans generation, born between 1925 and 1945, is also known as the World War II generation and traditionalists; many veterans have retired, while others are still working. Baby boomers, born between 1946 and 1963, are known mostly as baby boomers or boomers. Sometimes people born between 1962 and 1965 are called cuspers, since they were born in the years overlapping baby boomers and generation X. Generation X, born between 1963 and 1979, is sometimes called the 13th generation. Generation Y members were born between 1980 and 1994 and have many names: millennials, generation why?, echo boomers, 14th generation, Y2Kids, Internet generation, NetGeners or N-Gen, and Netizens. Members of Generation Z, born after 1995, are not yet working in libraries, but will be soon.[2]

Although the year ranges may shift slightly and the names and titles vary, library employees currently belong to one of four main generational groups: veterans, baby boomers, generation X, and generation Y.

Libraries, like other organizations and businesses, employ many baby boomers. In fact, baby boomers are the largest generation in the workforce today, with approximately 60.5 million workers in 1999, compared to 40 million generation Xers in the same year.[3] However, researchers believe that generation Y will become the largest generation ever.[4] Over the next few years, employers will need to rethink the traditional reward structure, adjusting to the increasingly generation X and generation Y workforce. While generational differences may influence the rewards desired by your employees, be careful not to let the stereotypes of each group determine reward options. Balancing the reward needs of four generations sounds impossible, but it doesn't have to be. Ask your staff what motivates them. You may be surprised by their answers.

Younger workers, for example, those born after 1964, might appreciate nonmonetary incentives or rewards such as increased responsibility, exposure to decision-makers, or more control over their own schedules.[5] Adding the supervision of student workers to a staff member's job description might be a reward to an employee wanting to build her skill set. An informal meeting with the library director, and the chance to tell the director about his new idea for streamlining the e-journal cataloging process, might be greatly appreciated by a technical services worker in a large library. The opportunity to work from home one day a week or to work a nontraditional schedule (10 a.m. to 7 p.m. instead of 8 a.m. to 5 p.m.) may help retain a high performer during years of lean raises.

If funding is available, consider purchasing rewards for these employees, rather than distributing a cash bonus. Generation X and generation Y employees may view additional training opportunities as a very worthwhile reward. If the training is job-related, the library will benefit as well. High-tech equipment which is job-related and which the employee would enjoy learning about and using, could also benefit the library. For example, providing a personal digital assistant (PDA) with a cell phone, camera, and wireless access for a library staff member working in your media lab, so that she can become familiar with the latest electronic gadgetry, would be a great reward. She has a high-tech PDA for her personal and work use and you have an employee with experience with the latest techno-gizmos.

Generation Y employees want to feel that their work has meaning, that they are making a difference. As a supervisor, you will need to find ways to convey to these young employees that their work does matter.

For generation X employees, freedom and balance are key. Xers want balance in their lives. They will work hard, and in return, they will feel rewarded by time off and flexible retirement options.

Baby boomers want recognition. Boomers want to work hard and do a good job, just like their veteran predecessors and parents, but they also want everyone to know how well they did it, whatever it is. They want the salary increase, company car, better work shift, etc., the proverbial corner office with a view. While most libraries have not provided company cars, the other examples, particularly office space and work shifts, do fit.

The expression "Hard work is its own reward" is familiar to most of us, even if we heard it from a parent rather than a coworker. For veterans, hard work is the ultimate reward. As the veteran generation ages, libraries might want to consider rewarding them with part-time, flextime, or work-from-home scheduling. Veteran employees will feel rewarded by being needed and valued in the workplace. Other traditional rewards such as a coffee mug, plaque, or a letter from the boss are also appreciated by this age group.

Figure 13-3 summarizes different reward approaches for different generations.

**FIGURE 13-3 ■ Different Rewards for Different Generations**

**Veterans/Traditionalists**

Handwritten thank-you note

Plaque

Photo of themselves with the library director (or college president, library board  president, important visitor, etc.)

Alternate scheduling

Job security

**Baby Boomers**

Time (errand service, dry cleaning pickup, etc.)

Promotion and new job title

Cash bonus

Expensive symbolic gift (Rolex watch, etc.)

Rewards that contribute toward plan for same standard of living at retirement

Retirement and financial counseling

**Generation X**

Challenging work

Higher salary and better benefits

Flexibility and freedom (work schedule)

Daily proof that work matters

Involvement in decision-making process

Managers who allow flexibility and creativity

Evidence of rewards tied directly to performance

Clear areas of responsibility

**Generation Y/Millennials/Nexters**

Meaningful work

Learning opportunities

Time for personal or family activities

A fun place to work

Desire for autonomy

Want to be treated like a colleague, not a kid

Fairness and fair play in the workplace

For groups, teams, and committees, the reward system should be tied to the group's goals and deadlines. When rewarding group members, identify the rewards that will motivate them—both individually and as a group—and then find ways to provide immediate rewards. For a team with members from multiple generations, offer a smorgasbord of rewards and let individuals choose. Rewarding the team members as they make progress, when they reach a milestone or meet a deadline, will motivate them to continue with the project.

For example, Sally heads a new, large technical services department in a library that restructured, merging three departments into one. The new department is composed primarily of baby boomers, with 75 percent of the staff in the baby boomer generation, 15 percent in the veterans group, 5 percent in generation X, and 5 percent in generation Y. Sally is a generation Xer who does not have much experience supervising baby boomers. She wants to set up a system to recognize those staff members who help develop procedures that will significantly streamline workflow and thereby free up staff to work on special projects. Her library has an incentive program to reward performance on task forces and projects. Sally decides to use the incentive program to encourage her staff to look creatively at the workflow. She calls a department meeting to announce the program. She plans to award an extra vacation day to staff who propose ideas that are then implemented. Her plan is met by silence. Sally is confused. What went wrong? Why isn't her new department energized by the plan?

After the meeting, Sally talks to a few of her staffers individually to get their reaction. She hears from two staff members in the veteran generation that they don't see any reason to reward ideas that should just be part of what good staff do. Why reward work that should be done anyway? Wouldn't a simple "Thank you" say it all? But Sally finds that her generation X colleagues like the idea of extra vacation days. They are already dreaming up plans to overhaul the unit. The baby boomers are not engaged in the project. Sally talks to a close friend in this generation who points out that not only do the majority of the members of the department expect to be included in the original planning of the incentive program, but that the incentives should include public recognition and acknowledgment of each person's role. Taking an extra vacation day may be pleasant, but it is not enough of an incentive to do the extra work.

Sally needs to regroup. She can give the department an opportunity to modify the incentive plan. She can include a project-end celebration and recognition party along with the vacation-day incentive. She can give staff a choice of two or three incentives rather than expecting everyone to want the same thing. By working with different members of the department, Sally can create a program to recognize and reward staff in ways that will be meaningful to most staff members.


## Conclusion

Appropriately rewarding and recognizing staff is an important component of the overall system for encouraging top performance by them. Look for ways to reward or recognize employees beyond salaries and wages, through both monetary and nonmonetary awards. Recognition programs should allow for different ways to reward staff members and should include a range of activities, from formal events to handwritten thank-you notes.

### NOTES

1. Irene M. Padilla and Thomas H. Patterson, "Rewarding Employees Nonmonetarily," in *Practical Help for New Supervisors,* ed. Joan Giesecke (Chicago: American Library Association, 1997), 36–38.

2. Scott Hays, "Generation X and the Art of the Reward," *Workforce* 11 (November 1999): 46; Lynne C. Lancaster and David Stillman, *When Generations Collide: Who They Are. Why They Clash. How to Solve the Generational Puzzle at Work* (New York: HarperCollins, 2002); Sue Schlichtemeier-Nutzman, presentation on multigenerational diversity for University Libraries, University of Nebraska-Lincoln, 2001.

3. Hays, "Generation X," 46.

4. Mark L. Alch, "Get Ready for a New Type of Worker in the Workplace: The Net Generation," *Supervision* 61 (April 2000): 3–7.

5. Ron Zemke, Claire Raines, and Bob Bilipczak, *Generations at Work: Managing the Clash of Veterans, Boomers, Xers, and Nexters in Your Workplace* (New York: AMACOM, 1999).

# 14

# Project Management

As the head of collection development, you arrive at work one day to find yourself asked to head a team to plan and identify 10 percent of the journal collection that can be eliminated in order to balance the budget. Your team will have six months to consult with interested groups and identify a clean list of titles that will be canceled. Every department in the library is affected by this budget problem, from selectors to reference staff to the technical services and systems staff. How will you go about ensuring that all these stakeholders are involved and still meet the short deadline for this project? You could decide to make all the decisions yourself, but you know that will not be effective. For one thing, you're not a subject expert in every area and you don't know all the intricacies of the various electronic licenses, package plans, and consortium purchases that will help determine which titles can actually be eliminated. Moreover, this is not the first time the library has had to cancel journals, and you know that the simpler decisions have already been made. This time you could be cutting core titles. What will you do? How can you organize this work and meet the deadline?

The preceding scenario is not all that unusual in today's libraries. Supervisors and managers may find themselves called upon to head interdepartmental projects or organization-wide task forces. When these assignments involve a project with a defined beginning and end, you may want to use a formal project management structure to organize and carry out the assignment. Project management is used extensively in the information technology field, where implementing new systems or resolving problems are often done as projects. Using a formal project management process will help you plan, organize, manage, and deliver projects with defined outcomes.[1]

Before you accept the assignment to head a project management work team, you will want to determine if project management is an appropriate process to use to structure the work. Are you being given a true project as the assignment? What is a project? A project is a planned undertaking and set of related activities that have a defined beginning and end. It is often an interdepartmental undertaking that includes resources that extend beyond one department. The scope of the project often affects many parts of the organization. While you can use a project management process within your own department, you may find it most helpful when working between organizational units.

## The Players

There are a number of people or stakeholders in the organization and outside of it that will be part of a project. Each group has a defined role in the process. Management is responsible for identifying projects, assigning priorities to projects, identifying the project manager, and providing on-going support. At the end of the project, management is responsible for recognizing and rewarding the project manager and team.

The sponsor of the project is the member of the management team who authorizes the project, grants the project manager the authority to complete the project, and supports the project manager throughout the life of the project. The sponsor is responsible for finding the resources needed by the team to accomplish the charge.

The project manager is the person who heads the project team and controls the processes that make the project happen. The project manager negotiates for time and resources needed by the team. Being a project manager can turn into a full-time job. The project manager needs to negotiate for changes in his or her own work assignments in order to be sure to have time to devote to the project.

The project team consists of the people who are responsible for doing the work. These people are chosen by the project manager based on the skills needed by the team to carry out the charge to the group.

Customers or users are the groups that will be affected in some way by the outcomes of the project. In the journal cancellation project, users can include the faculty and students in a school or academic environment, the library users in a public setting, or the members of a company for a special library.

As part of the planning process, the project team will want to be sure to identify as many of the stakeholders as it can. This way the team can be sure that groups that need to be consulted or informed about the project will receive appropriate and timely communication.

## Managing the Project Process

There are four phases to a project: initiating the project, planning the project, executing the project, and closing down the project. It is important to be sure to go through all four phases, including closing down the project, in order to have a successful project.

### Project Initiation

In the initial phase of the project, the size, scope, and complexity of the project are identified. As the project manager, you will want to use this time to establish the parameters of the project, choose the project team, and negotiate your authority, your time commitment, and the resources you will have available to you. For your own survival, be sure you negotiate which of your regular responsibilities you will not be fulfilling so that you will have time to devote to the project.

Choosing your project team is a crucial step in creating a successful venture. Work with the sponsor of the project to identify the skills that are needed for the project. Then choose members of the organization who have the skills you need. Look for people who can complement your strengths.

Review the charge to the team with the sponsor. Be sure you understand exactly what is being asked of the group and agree to the outcomes. How will you know if you are successful? For the journal cancellation project, be sure you know exactly what journal cost total is 10 percent of the budget. Since journal costs change every year, be sure you agree on how you will determine the subscription cost for a given title. Iron out any differences now before you begin the project. This will avoid problems later on in the project.

Outline the steps needed to begin the project. Who needs to be contacted as part of the initiation phase? How will you report to the sponsor and other members of the management group? How will you assign roles to team members? How will you work with the sponsor if changes are needed in the project? What type of funding can you expect for the project? These are the kinds of questions you want to be sure are answered as part of the initiation phase.

Finally in this initial stage, establish how you will keep track of the correspondence, activities, and deliverables that are part of the project. Creating a project notebook, either in print or online, can help you keep the group and the procedures organized. It will be important to record decisions made, communications sent, and reports submitted throughout the process. Establishing how you will document your progress now will make it easier to keep track of the project throughout its lifetime.

### Project Planning

There are six basic steps for planning a project: defining the objectives, structuring the project, scheduling the project, analyzing the plan for risks, reviewing the plan for assumptions, and establishing controls.

*Define the objectives.* Define the scope of the project. What is the problem to be solved? What are the deliverables (i.e., expected results) for this project and how will they be measured? How will you know when the project is finished? These questions need to be answered as a first step in the planning process. In the journal cancellation project, you will want to know what information needs to be included in the list of journals. Do you need ISSN numbers, costs, publisher information, vendor information, or just a list of journal titles? Will the list be in a spreadsheet format, done from an online system, or handwritten? Working out these details now will help ensure that you don't need to redo work once it has been done.

*Structure the project.* Now is the time to divide the project into manageable tasks. Identify the tasks to be accomplished and the order in which they will be done. These are known as work breakdown structures and help you develop a logical approach to the work that will need to be done.

Part of the planning process includes developing a communication plan. Often this is the step we are most likely to skip or do quickly. However, having a well-thought-out communication plan can be the difference between a successful project and one with problems. In the communication plan, include when and how reports on progress will be given and to whom. How will stakeholders be consulted? Will publicity for the project be needed? If so, who will do the publicity and when? In the journal cancellation project, consider how you will announce the plan to your constituencies. How will you alert users that journals will be canceled? How will you keep the members of the staff informed of your progress so they can answer questions from patrons about the project? The more you communicate and follow a careful plan for communicating, the fewer problems you will have with misinformation getting out and rumors destroying your progress or credibility.

*Schedule the project.* Now that you have the tasks identified, estimate the resources you will need to accomplish those tasks. Resources include staff time as well as budget resources, supplies, and equipment needed for the project. You should also identify the amount of time needed for each task. Some tasks may need to be accomplished before others can begin. Some tasks may be able to be done simultaneously. Some tasks can be accomplished more quickly by increasing the resources devoted to them. Identify those tasks that are most critical and be sure you have allowed enough time to accomplish them. Get agreement for the budget and timeline from your sponsor or management group.

*Assess risks.* Now that you have the tasks listed and a schedule in mind, assess the risks involved in the project. What happens if an internal deadline is missed? How likely is it that supplies or equipment could be delayed? How likely is it that the project will result in adverse publicity for the organization? How can you decrease the chances of various problems occurring? Are there things you can do in your plan to decrease any particular risk from becoming a problem?

*Review the plan for assumptions.* Can the timeline be met? Are the resources you need available? Can the work be done as outlined in the plan? Think about the assumptions you made when developing the task list and be sure they are still valid.

*Establish controls.* Negotiate the budget and the plan with management. Review the key statement of work with the sponsor and be sure that the key stakeholders have a clear understanding of what you plan to do and how you plan to do it. Be sure everyone understands the project size, duration, and outcomes. Finally, determine how you will make changes in the plan as needed and how you will keep the sponsor and management group informed of changes as they occur.

Once you have reviewed and agreed to a plan of action, you are ready to execute the project.

### Project Execution

Now is the time to follow your plan. Initiate activities, assign resources, train staff as needed, and assure that quality measures are being met. You may need to do some team-building here to be sure that those involved in the project work well together as a team that is dependent on each member meeting their assignments.

Monitor progress on each task and be sure your team members are doing the work they said they would do. Continually compare progress on activities to the baseline plan and be sure you are on target. Adjust resource allocations as needed if budgets get ahead or behind schedule. Reassign personnel if needed to meet the project deadlines.

Make changes and adjustments as needed to keep the project on track. You may need to change specifications or internal deadlines or redo activities if a task gets bungled. Also identify new activities that may be needed but were not anticipated in the planning process. For example, in the journal cancellation project, you may need to add in meetings with interested faculty if you had not included them initially and the faculty become more concerned than anticipated. Finally, decide what to do if an activity is delayed. Can you rearrange tasks, adjust schedules, or move resources to bring the project back on track? Be sure you are maintaining the project workbook and documenting progress throughout the project.

### Project Closedown

You have finished your tasks, met your deadlines, and are ready to end the project. Be sure you formally close down the project so everyone will know that you are done. Notify stakeholders that the project is concluded and deliverables have been finished. Work with management and customers to assess the strengths and weaknesses of the deliverables. Have you provided the final product that was needed? Can the organization use the work you did?

In addition to ending the tasks, you need to close down the team. Assess your team members, and support their transitions back to their regular jobs. Finalize documentation and submit budget reports that are required. And most important, celebrate your success. You have done a great job and deserve to celebrate that success. The celebration is also a way for the organization to thank all of the team members for their help in making the project a success.

## Conclusion

By following a formal planning and project process, you can manage both large and small projects and bring them to successful outcomes. Skipping steps or cutting short the process will increase the chances of failure. Instead take the time needed to do the project correctly and thoroughly. In the end you will save time and resources that would otherwise be needed to redo the work Project management can be very satisfying and fun. When done well it can help you accomplish complex, interdepartmental tasks and show management that you are a successful project manager.

### NOTE

1. There are numerous books that outline the formal project management process. For an overview of the process, see Patricia Buhler, *Alpha Teach Yourself Management Skills in 24 Hours* (Indianapolis, Ind.: Alpha Books, 2001), 83–98; and George M. Doss, *IS Project Management Handbook* (New York: Prentice Hall, 2000).

# 15
# Career Management

While you are busy supporting the development of your staff and helping them plan their careers, it is also important to take time to plan your own career. But before you sigh and decide that this is one more ball you don't want to juggle, take a moment to think about where you are in your career and where you want to be. Even if you have addressed your career goals, it's important to be aware of changes in the field, in your organization, and in your life that can affect your position and change how you feel about your career. Keeping an eye on your career can help you achieve balance between your personal and your work life.

Career management has changed. In the last generation, a career implied working for one organization. Employees spent thirty or more years with the same organization and did not consider changing jobs. Today, we live in a world where many of our staff will have three or four careers and will move among fields. Job-switching is becoming more common. Employees look for ways to stay engaged, refreshed, and challenged. If their current job does not keep them excited, they leave. You may feel the same way. If so, you can take steps to keep your career moving forward.

## Stages of Career Development

Traditionally, careers proceeded through the following stages: exploration, organizational entry, establishment, maintenance, and finally, disengagement.[1] You started by learning about a career area, usually through higher education options. Perhaps you worked in a library as a student. You found out more about the field and the job options for librarians and information scientists.

Next, you find a job in this field. The challenge here is to match your own interests and skills with that of an employer. Finding a satisfying first job can be a real challenge. Once the first job is acquired, you need to build the skills that will make you a valuable employee.

As time goes on, you will reach a midcareer level. Here is a time to assess where you are in your career. Are you satisfied with the skills you have? Do you enjoy what you do? If not, it's time to make changes. If you are satisfied with your career, then be sure to examine how you can keep your skills current and continue to grow in our constantly changing information environment.

The final stage of a career is retirement or disengagement. Here you want to look at what new things you want to do and how you will change your life by either retiring or starting a new career.

While these are the traditional steps in career development, people entering the workforce now may have three, four, or more careers in their lifetime. Their planning time frame will be shorter, but they will still experience these four stages of career development.

## Nonlinear Career Paths

The process just described is a linear approach to career development. It looks good on paper but may not relate to your experience. Instead, we need to recognize that there are a variety of career paths open to us. These include upward mobility, project management, resource provider, and technical advancement.[2]

Upward mobility is the traditional career path for managers. You start as a first-time supervisor and advance through the management ranks. This path still exists, but the number of positions in this path is decreasing. As organizations merge, restructure, and downsize, management opportunities are eliminated. As a manager, you will want to carefully watch what is happening to jobs in your area and prepare for changes.

Project management provides a different advancement option for today's supervisors. Project managers oversee significant projects and contribute to the success of the organization. Leading projects can be a way to advance in your organization even though you do not head a unit or department.

Obtaining financial resources is another career opportunity. These are the people who manage and obtain resources, and oversee the human relations aspects of the organization. This staff function can be a career advancement opportunity.

Technical expertise is another way to promote advancement. Technical experts possess knowledge, skills, and abilities that help the organization remain technologically current and enable it to advance in our changing field.[3]

## Plateaus

Career plateaus can occur even when you have carefully planned your approach to career development. Structural plateaus occur when there are no promotional opportunities left in your current organization. Here, your option for upward mobility is limited to finding positions in other organizations.[4]

Content plateaus occur when you have mastered the tasks of your position and find you have no more challenges. Content plateaus are less likely to occur in the information field, where changes in technology and in information resources add interest and change to our positions. Opportunities for learning abound in our field.

Another source of plateauing can occur when we feel we can no longer advance and see this lack of change as a failure in our lives. Staff who measure their self-identity by their jobs can be vulnerable to such feelings. As a manager, you want to be sure you don't become so focused on your job that you neglect other areas of your life.

## Personal Guidance

To manage your career, you should decide where you want to go and then design strategies to get there. You may want to carry out your own strategic planning process for your career.

Begin with a vision just as you do for your organization or unit. Describe what kinds of positions you want. Where do you want to be in five or ten years? What aspects of the information field are most exciting to you? What jobs do you see around you that look interesting and exciting?

Decide too, what kind of organizations you want to work in. Do you prefer small organizations, multibranch systems, large organizations, or commercial, nonprofit, or public institutions? Thinking through the characteristics of an organization that is important to you will help you map out your career.

Next, it's time to do your own SWOT analysis of your Strengths, Weaknesses, Opportunities, and Threats. Look at what skills you have and which ones you need to develop. Think about the options you have to build your career and the barriers that can slow your progress.

Use this information to help focus your planning so you can capitalize on opportunities when they arrive. Look for projects that will help you gain experience that rounds out your skill set. Add to and refine your options as you assess changes in the larger organization or environment that can affect your own goals.

And finally, stay flexible. The information field is always changing. Jobs change and organizations change. If you are too rigid in your planning, you may miss opportunities to advance or may become stuck in a dead-end position.

## Avoiding Dead Ends

You can work to avoid dead-end positions if you keep your eyes open and pay attention to how the information field is developing.[5]

*Trends.* Keep up with the literature about the information field. Read what trends, changes, and new options are developing. By staying aware of how the field is changing, you can assess how to use these changes to your advantage.

*Technology.* Keep current on technology changes. As our patrons move from computers to laptops to PDAs for their information, we need to move with them. Even if your library isn't keeping up with the latest technology and software advances, you need to be aware of these changes. By keeping your skills current, you will stay more employable and better able to control your own career options.

*Networking.* You also want to be sure you continue to network with colleagues, other managers, vendors, etc., even as you move through management positions. Your personal network can help you assess your career options as well as help alert you to changes that may be harmful to your own advancement.

*Mergers and reorganizations.* Finally, be aware that mergers and reorganizations can occur and can change the direction your career is taking. Library systems can merge, and certain types of libraries are now merging or downsizing. Schools and corporations may be eliminating their libraries. While you cannot anticipate every possible change, you can stay prepared for changes by watching for signs of financial or other problems and by watching how top decision-makers are assessing the organization. As you learn to read between the lines on announcements of changes, you can prepare yourself for more changes to come. By keeping your skills up-to-date and your options open, you will have a better chance of surviving an economic downturn or a major restructuring effort.

## Personal Balance

While you work on your career plans, you should also look at how to achieve a balance in your life. Personal health, family happiness, and work effectiveness are all related. You are more effective at work when you take care of your own well-being and develop a positive life outside of your job.[6]

You can apply the same planning techniques you use to assess your career to planning your personal life. Begin by identifying your personal values. Decide what things are most important to you. Think about how you rank social interactions, friends, family, religious values, a home, time for recreation, etc. Decide too, how you like to spend your time. How much time do you want or need for work, sleep, social activities, home maintenance, etc.? Putting these two lists together will help you focus your time.

Next, set realistic goals for yourself, given the things you need to do and want to do. Use these goals to design your own personal action plan of how you will spend your time. If refereeing your children's softball games is a high priority, then look at how to arrange your job so you have time to be a referee. If serving on a local charity board is a goal, think about what steps you need to take to become a member of the board.

And then leave yourself time for fun and relaxation. Try to remember that you cannot control every minute of your day. Do take time to enjoy yourself, to refresh and relax. This time will help you stay refreshed and more able to cope with the challenges at work and in your personal life.

## Managing Stress

No matter how well you take care of yourself, you will find yourself under pressure and will experience stress. One key to surviving the pressures of everyday life is to learn to manage that stress as best you can. There are numerous techniques or rules that can help you deal with stress in a constructive manner.

First, take a deep breath and recognize that you cannot always be right. Mistakes do happen. Other people have better ideas. Instead of trying to always be right, try to do your best and accept that sometimes you will not be first, nor will you always be the best.

Second, don't let stresses build up. Handle little situations as they occur to prevent larger problems later on. For example, don't wait until the last minute to start a project. Set up a timeline that lets you work on a project and that allows for problems to arise and be handled before the deadline. By planning in time for problems, you can decrease the stress that is caused by rushing to meet a deadline when things go awry.

Last, learn what situations cause you stress and develop strategies for handling these situations. For example, if you know you become stressed if you are late for an appointment, then plan your day to try to arrive ten minutes early. That way if something comes up that delays you, you are still likely to be on time for the meeting. By studying your own reactions to different situations, you can learn to control your reactions and behavior. You can decrease stress by decreasing the number of times you are surprised or caught off guard.

Stress is a natural part of our lives. By learning to manage stress, you can decrease the effects it has on your life, your health, and your work.

## Conclusion

Remember to take time to take care of yourself and your career. Think carefully about how to balance your personal life and your work life. Develop goals and plans that help you meet your own needs as you work to ensure that your staff and unit meet the organization's needs. You will not be effective if you neglect your own life, become frustrated, and get burned out. Instead, take time to reflect and plan so you can enjoy your life and your career.

## NOTES

**1.** Patricia Buhler, *Alpha Teach Yourself Management Skills in 24 Hours* (Indianapolis, Ind.: Alpha Books, 2001), 188.

**2.** Ibid., 191.

**3.** Ibid.

**4.** Ibid., 190.

**5.** Gary McClain and Deborah Romaine, *The Everything Managing People Book* (Avon, Mass.: Adams Media, 2002), 261–81.

**6.** Edward Betoff and Frederic Harwood, *Just Promoted* (New York: McGraw-Hill, 1992), 233.

# INDEX

**Joan Giesecke** is dean of libraries at the University of Nebraska–Lincoln. She joined the university in 1987 and became dean in 1996. Prior to this, she held positions at George Mason University, Prince George's County Memorial Library System, and the American Health Care Association. She received a doctorate in public administration from George Mason University, an M.L.S. degree from the University of Maryland, and a master's degree in management from Central Michigan University. Giesecke is a former editor of *Library Administration and Management* and has published numerous articles on management issues. Her books include *Practical Help for New Supervisors* (1997), *Scenario Planning for Libraries* (1998), and *Practical Strategies for Library Managers* (2001).

**Beth McNeil** is associate dean of libraries at the University of Nebraska–Lincoln, where she has responsibility for the overall management of technical services operations, coordinates the staff development program, coordinates librarywide statistics efforts, and manages librarywide special projects. Prior to coming to the University of Nebraska–Lincoln, McNeil was head of reference services at Bradley University in Peoria, Illinois. She received an M.S. degree in library and information science from the University of Illinois at Urbana-Champaign. Her books include *Patron Behavior in Libraries* (1996) and *Human Resource Management in Today's Academic Library* (2004).